W9-AMT-890

School Smarts
The Four Cs of Academic Success

Jim Burke

HEINEMANN
Portsmouth, NH

Heinemann

A division of Reed Elsevier Inc.

361 Hanover Street

Portsmouth, NH 03801–3912

www.heinemann.com

Offices and agents throughout the world

The author and publisher wish to thank those who have generously given permission to reprint borrowed material:

Excerpt from *The Connected Classroom Solution Definition,* pp. 12–14, by G.T. Springer. Internal document copyright Texas Instruments 2003.

Figure 1.1: Graph of responses from professors and employers reprinted by permission of Public Agenda.

Figure 5.1: "Apprenticeship Model" by Ruth Schoenbach. Copyright © 1996 by Ruth Schoenbach. Updated version can be found in *Building Academic Literacy: Lessons from Reading Apprenticeship Classrooms* by Ruth Schoenbach. Reprinted by permission of the author.

Figure 6.2: from *Educational Care, 2/e* by Melvin D. Levine. Copyright © 1994 by Melvin D. Levine. Reprinted by permission of Educators Publishing Service, 625 Mt. Auburn Street, Cambridge MA, (800) 225-5750, www.epsbooks.com.

Figures 7.2a, b: "Cycle of Inquiry" by Nancy Sullivan. Copyright © 2003 by Bay Area School Reform Collaborative. Used by permission. All rights reserved.

"Study Guide for Biology" by George Kodros. Used by permission of the author.

"Study Guide for History" by Steve Mills. Used by permission of the author.

"Teaming Up for Success" by Sabrina Crawford. Copyright © 2003 by Sabrina Crawford. Reprinted by permission of the author.

Appendix B: "Executive Summary of the English Literacy Publication" was published by The Intersegmental Committee of Academic Senates. Reprinted by permission.

Library of Congress Cataloging-in-Publication Data

Burke, Jim.

   School smarts : the four Cs of academic success / Jim Burke.

     p. cm.

   Includes bibliographical references and index.

   ISBN 0-325-00632-6

   1. Academic achievement.   2. Learning.   I. Title.

LB1060.B87 2004

373.13'028'1—dc22   2004009668

Editor: Lois Bridges

Production: Abigail M. Heim

Interior design: Joni Doherty Design

Typesetter: Kim Arney Mulcahy

Cover coordinator: Renée Le Verrier

Cover photography: Bruce Forrester, Bruce Forrester Photography, Inc.

Cover design: Judy Arisman, Arisman Design Studio

Manufacturing: Steve Bernier

About the Cover: Tony Arteaga, shown in consultation with the author, was the winner of the Cultura Latina College Scholarship and the College of San Mateo Scholarship from Burlingame High School during his senior year; fifteen scholarships were awarded to seniors from Burke's ACCESS program at Burlingame that year.

Printed in the United States of America on acid-free paper

08   07   06   05   04   EB   1   2   3   4   5

To my students, for all they teach me about school and life,

and to Tom Nieman, friend, colleague, mentor

Education! Which of the various me's do you propose to educate?

—D. H. Lawrence

A traveler in a foreign land best learns names of people and places, how to express ideas, ways to carry on a conversation by moving around in the culture, participating as fully as he can, making mistakes, saying things half-right, blushing, then being encouraged by a friendly native speaker to try again.

—Mike Rose, *Lives on the Boundary*

Contents

![cccc]

Acknowledgments

For four years I have been involved in a conversation with teachers around the country about the question of academic success and how those of us in the schools—whether teachers or administrators—can help students achieve it. It is the central question we all face as we move deeper into the work of helping all students succeed in school and life, in the classroom and at work, on class assignments and state tests. Throughout the journey of the last few years I have relied on many people, some of them students, others colleagues, still others fellow writers. I am grateful to them all for their teachings.

Every day I go to work at Burlingame High School, a place I have called home for eleven years now. I am particularly grateful for the contributions the following colleagues at Burlingame High made to this book through conversations, example, or guidance: Matt Biggar, Sandy Briggs, Jean Marie Buckley, Elaine Caret, Jackie Estes, Frank Firpo, Sue Glick, John Harris, Karen Latham, Diane McClain, Steve Mills, Mario Mora, Beth Pascal, Michelle Riley, Rebecca Shirley, Bill Smith, and Matt Vaughn.

Many authors have informed and inspired me, but several whom I have come to know and have been able to consult deserve special mention: Sam Intrator, Denise Clark Pope, Robert Marzano, Jay Mathews, Erin Gruwell, Carol Jago, Judith Langer, and Tom Newkirk. To this list, I must add a special note of gratitude to a few authors whose work was essential, but whom I do not know. First among these colleagues is Mike Rose, whose book *Lives on the Boundary* no doubt began the conversation within me that this book continues. Magdalene Lampert's book *Teaching Problems and the Problems of Teaching* inspired crucial connections and helped me better understand the whole concept of academic identity in new ways. *Learning Outside the Lines*, a book by Jonathan Mooney and David Cole, takes the lid off of the whole academic enterprise and shows us what it's all about and how to succeed in that sometimes vicious culture of schools. And finally, the authors of *Reading for Understanding* (Ruth Schoenbach, Cynthia Greenleaf, Christine Cziko, and Lori Hurwitz), the book that is most responsible for the current discussion about and emphasis on academic literacy.

It's nice to learn from scholars and colleagues, but when it comes to the messy, fascinating business of teaching, no one has more to offer than the kids themselves. I do my best to learn from all my students, but those in my ACCESS (Academic Success) program have offered me the most important insights into school success. In particular, I wish to thank the following students: Tony Arteaga, Brian Blanton, Maricela Vega, Jorge Rodriguez, Lourdes Toloza, Zaniesha Woods, Paulina Gavilanez, Lisa Marconi, Samantha Marconi, Allison Molina, Benjamin Pierce, Gina San Pietro, Danny Martin, Eduardo Pena, Francesca Umli, Nelson Tejada, and Danielle Franco.

Others play crucial roles and I cannot pass up the opportunity to thank them for their contribution to this book and its ideas: Tom Nieman, and the reading teachers in the San Mateo Union High School District, including Joan Rossi; Leigh Peake, Mike Gibbons, Abby Heim, Renée Le Verrier, Maura Sullivan, Kären Clausen, Brita Mess, Pat Carls, Eric Chalek, and Steve Bernier. Of all my many guides, none offers more support, insight, and intelligence than my editor, Lois Bridges; indeed, I think of all of my books as *our* books, for the conversation between us inevitably helps shape and refine my ideas so that they are clearer than I could ever make them myself.

Finally, I must thank my family for their support. Given the nature of this book, my own children, especially Evan and Whitman, who are now in middle and elementary school, contributed to this book in important ways as I watched them work and listened to their thoughts about school. My wife, Susan, listens to, questions, and contributes to all I write; I cannot ever thank her enough for her support. And I must thank my own parents, who are part of the story I have told here: they have taught me for nearly forty-three years now; long after my father's death, his words and example continue to teach me.

A Personal Prologue: The Student I Was, the Student I Became, the Teacher I Am

I try never to let schooling get in the way of my education.

—Mark Twain

Dear Mr. and Mrs. Burke:

This letter is to inform you that your son Jim Burke will be ineligible to graduate or to participate in the graduation ceremonies on June 8th unless he passes his English class. Enclosed you will find a copy of his most recent progress report and his current transcript. His teacher, Mr. Kitchener, has informed us that Jim's grade in his senior English class as of June 3rd is an F. He must pass this class, as it is a graduation requirement; it is also the last five units he needs to achieve the required number of units to graduate.

Students who do not have the required 210 units in the proper subject areas will not participate in the graduation ceremony. Students can complete any graduation deficits over the summer to earn a diploma. Should you have any questions, please do not hesitate to call me.

Sincerely,
Bruce Wells
Counselor

I would like to be able to tell you that when this letter arrived in the last weeks of my high school career, I was working hard on the latest assignment I had decided not to do; the truth, however, is that I was lounging by the pool in our backyard with my friends Dave and Doug, both of whom were heading off to college in the fall.

When my mother erupted out of the house waving the letter in her hand, I already knew something was up: I could hear her voice from the front hall, where she had stood reading the letter that capped years of academic mediocrity and, at times, failure.

"What the hell is this all about?" she demanded as Dave and Doug dove into the pool for a little refreshment—and distance.

"Oh . . . *that*? I thought they said they weren't going to send that. It's all taken care of, Mom. I swear. I didn't turn that project into Ken [my English teacher, who insisted we call him by his first name] on time, so he hadn't graded it. He said he'd grade it this weekend. Not to worry, Mom."

"It better be squared away, that's all I have to say." With that, she retreated to the cool interior of the house, leaving me to wonder how I would get out of such a mess this time. Doug and Dave both propped themselves up on the edge of the pool, grinning, shaking their heads at a me, saying only that their parents would kill them if they got into such a situation.

Over the next week I would consult with Ken—ironically, the teacher most responsible for me becoming a teacher—about my standing, asking what I could do to pass his class. It's a conversation those of you reading this know too well. And ultimately it worked out: I received the "gift D–" I needed to walk the stage. The problem was that on the other side of that stage stood the realization that all my friends were leaving for college by summer's end to begin preparing for a future I had never allowed myself to consider.

As my transcript shows (see Figure 1), I drifted between what appealed to me and what the school required.

My poor academic performance was by no means limited to senior year or even high school. I can still see my great friend John Russell and myself trying to "fix" our middle school report cards so that the Ds resembled Bs—*sort of*. I spent much more time in middle school trying to see the legendary hickies on Renee Mell's neck than trying to jot down what Mr. Longwell told us about math or Mrs. Cook said about history as she stood straight and stared at the red dot on the back wall, so uncomfortable was she about speaking in front of groups. When I wasn't doctoring report cards or speculating about Renee's neck, I was playing basketball or waiting to get into the woodshop to work on my lathe projects, which offered a pleasant calm in the middle of an otherwise disorienting day.

Only one teacher stands out in my mind from middle school: Mr. Rothshiller, the hardest, most demanding, and most unique teacher in the whole school. He taught zoology, had arms covered with tattoos, had been a boxer, and demanded more of students than all the other teachers combined. You knew you were in for it on those days when you entered his class and saw the

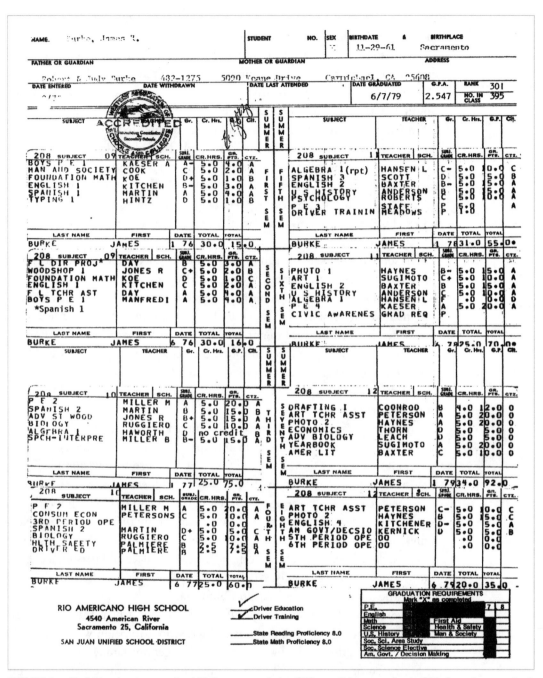

FIGURE 1. My high school transcript. While my cumulative GPA was 2.5, my academic GPA (based on required academic classes) was 1.7. It's worth noting that my sister, three years younger than I am, held approximately the same class rank and earned an even lower GPA (but, alas, earned much higher rankings in tennis than I did).

dreaded skull perched atop his desk: this meant a pop quiz on something like the bones of the hand or the respiratory system of sharks.

Something in me responded to Mr. Rothshiller: he was one of those teachers you wanted to please, whose opinion of you mattered, and who asked you to go inside yourself and find the stuff needed to do what he asked. Try as I might, however, I lacked the academic sensibilities that told others which pieces of information mattered most, or how to solve a complicated problem such as dissecting a shark and then displaying it, properly labeled, and *without* formaldehyde dripping all over the posterboard. Tests were just another chance to fail, as they would be through much of high school. Somehow school smarts seemed a genetic gift I had not received. My dad taught me how to build and fix things, how to hunt and fish, how to throw a curveball, but somehow note taking and test taking never got onto our menu.

In some misguided effort to prove my intelligence to both Mr. Rothshiller and myself, I spent an entire weekend holed up in my room staring at what passed for notes so that I might not just pass but excel on the next test. Lacking any method, any strategies, any sense of my own mind and how it learned, I was beaten before I began. I might as well have been down at the river hunting lizards or riding my motorcycle through the fields that surrounded our house. When I failed the big zoology test that prevented me from continuing on in the class, I did not pitch a fit or cry; I probably went home and watched television or rode my motorcycle.

By eighth grade, however, something entered my life that would eventually change me in ways I could not then anticipate: tennis. Everything else became irrelevant as I sought to master this sport that I had somehow stumbled upon one Saturday morning when my buddy Wayne Schloemer asked me if I wanted to go play tennis. From the age of eleven until the end of high school, despite failure or general lack of direction in other areas of my life, I devoted myself to tennis with a passion that gave my life a sense of purpose and let me taste success on a daily basis. It established my identity as a successful person, a competent person, a feeling I rarely experienced in school. Eventually I would rank among the top fourteen-year-olds in California.

Meanwhile, I was also beginning high school when I was fourteen. Though my father had dropped out of high school to begin working for the Office of State Printing, he had worked hard to get our family into nicer parts of Sacramento, hoping that better schools could make the difference in our lives that they did not in his when he was younger. My mother provided a different example, but one no less influential: a high school graduate who had her first child (me) at nineteen, she pursued her interest in real estate, locking herself away in their bedroom to study for her license, a process of intense self-education and focused study that culminated in her success on the test and in the business.

Ours was not a literate household in the same way my friend Micky's was. His father, who was a doctor, routinely sat at the kitchen table, where all could see him reading articles, journals, newspapers, contracts, and stock reports. Micky grew up surrounded by expectations that he would go to college, swathed in reminders of the importance of doing well in school, and supported in those endeavors early on by parents and siblings who offered resources, guidance, strategies, and whatever else was needed to help him succeed in school. In elementary school Mick focused on school, while John Russell and I planned out how many suckers we should buy after school to sell the next day, or while I used my budding writing skills to court girls, asking Kim Simmons if she wanted to "go study with me," by which I meant "go steady." Thus began the first of many two-week school relationships that would prepare me for the day, years later, when I would write the woman I would eventually marry, asking her to "stop by and visit me in Tunisia," where I was serving in the Peace Corps; she was living in Japan at the time and I had not yet addressed my gross lack of geographical knowledge. No doubt Kim Simmons, reading my note of proposal, thought, as my wife did when she read my note in Japan, "He's a nice guy. Not too bright, but nice."

In many respects, this sums up the way I saw myself and others saw me during the high school years: nice and not too bright. I had no real sense of what it was all for, what it led to, how it might help me. Some ask me if I was just bored, felt uninspired or not challenged; but this just wasn't the case. As my report card shows, I showed up and behaved well (thus getting good-citizenship grades) and rarely did my work. I had no real sense of how to do the work I was asked to complete; so much of it seemed to require skills and capacities that I lacked. When friends like Micky turned their work in, on time, done well, it just confirmed my own sense that I was not cut out for academic work. In biology, when assigned a big group project, I had no idea how to approach such work, leaving it to greater minds to tell me what to do.

No matter how badly I did in school, however, I was unable to see myself as incompetent for the simple fact that I had an area—tennis—that earned me others' respect and established that I could do something well. The only problem was that during my junior year of high school, I grew restless and eventually stopped playing competitive tennis. This would be the logical place in this abbreviated memoir to describe my academic awakening, to tell about the day when the clouds parted and I realized that everything I did to master tennis—repetitive drills to improve my skills, weightlifting and running to develop my strength and stamina, *even reading books* about the great tennis players to learn their secrets—could help me master school. Instead of turning my attention to school, however, I did what many kids do at that age: got my first girlfriend, got my driver's license, got a job (at the Bubble Machine car wash, where my flawed mathematical skills earned me the weekly privilege of cleaning out the trough that collected the dirt from all the cars), hung out with my friends—and did not do my schoolwork. Occasionally I played at being a student, the most memorable time being when I signed up to take the PSAT. I did this because my buddies, who were all college-bound, were taking it. I did not prepare for it; in fact, the night before the test turned out to be an unfortunate and untimely rite of passage: getting drunk for the first time at a party. I was so hung over the morning of the PSAT that I had to run out of the cafeteria before even completing the personal information page.

Ironically, this crucial failure led to an important but brief awakening. After running out of the cafeteria and getting sick behind the woodshop building, I fell asleep under the tree outside my English teacher's room. On that Saturday, while the good children of my high school tackled the PSAT and dreamt of their future, I slept until the sun woke me hours later. The test was over and everyone was long gone. Instead of going home, I did something that still amazes me: I went to my locker and retrieved *Bless the Beasts and the Children*, which I was supposed to be reading in English, then sat down under the tree outside Mr. Baxter's class and read—and read, and read, as I never had before. Hours later, having lost myself in that book, I lifted my head up to realize it was getting on toward dinner and my parents had no idea where I was. After returning the book to my locker, I began the long walk home.

You already know from the opening that my conversion did not last long. By the end of my senior year, I was ranked 301st out of 365 students and had an academic GPA of 1.7. After graduating, I took a job working in a printing shop downtown, where I spent my days working alongside women who lived to smoke cigarettes, drink Coke, and talk about soap operas before going back to the table where we stood folding and stuffing envelopes with brochures for weekend vacations none of us would ever be able to afford. As soon as I got off work the first week, I headed south to visit my friend Micky at the University of the Pacific, where he was just beginning his freshman year. Driving back home after the weekend, thinking about what his life—and mine—was like, I decided it was time to see what school had to offer, and so that Monday I headed straight to American River Community College when I clocked out, and registered for classes.

Over the course of the next year I began to realize how complex school is, how demanding academic study is. I had no idea how to take notes during lectures or what to do while I read. So I began to watch others. Everyone else had highlighters, so I got one. The problem was that I thought every sentence was important, so I highlighted them all. I would have been better off reading with a can of spray paint; honestly, I highlighted whole pages. Only later did I realize how useless this was. I began to ask others if I could see their notes, to learn from them what was essential to write down and how to organize it on the page. My mind was something like a balloon that was being stretched for the first time; thus it became more elastic, more flexible, more capacious. I began to understand how academic classes worked, to recognize the different demands they made on writers, readers, thinkers, and speakers. Still, it was a slow process, as evidenced by my professor's response to my paper on *Hamlet*. He simply crossed out the front page and wrote in three-inch-high letters: "So what?!" Eventually I gathered up the courage to visit him during his office hours, something I hadn't realized you could do. This conference led to the beginning of a relationship that would help sustain me through that first year, a relationship that taught me to ask for what I needed to succeed and to take the necessary risks to achieve that success. Throughout this process, I had to learn not only about sociology but sociology professors; not just economics but listening, note taking, and test taking. Gradually my investment began to show returns: I earned Cs on papers and tests and could learn from those mistakes so I could do better next time. By the time I transferred to a four-year college, where I found professors like Dr. Triplet—he could draw and write with both hands simultaneously on the overhead, while explaining the concepts out loud—I was ready, but only because people began to teach me the culture, language, and customs of this strange new country called School.

I still lacked a full understanding of the purpose of education. Having come from a family in which no one had ever graduated from college, I thought you went to college to make money, which is why I majored in economics—until a summer job with kids revealed that my gifts lay elsewhere. By the time I graduated from college, I was already teaching kids with developmental disabilities. Soon thereafter I joined the Peace Corps and went to teach similar kids in Tunisia, an experience that required me to learn to speak Arabic, but by that point I knew how I learned. More important, I knew that I *could* learn. Two years later, having created a small school in the back of a mosque for kids with learning difficulties, I came home and completed the courses needed to become an English teacher, which is all I dreamt of doing after reading on my verandah in Tunisia those last two years.

The story ends where it began: students much like myself arriving at Castro Valley High School, where I began my teaching career, not knowing how to "do school," most of them from families like mine, some from other countries, and all of them wanting the same thing—success in school and in life. On occasion, during heated discussions in class, a student might ask me about my own faith, about what I believe in; my answer to this question has always been the same: I believe in education.

ONE
Introduction
Understanding Academic Success

When we enter a house for the first time, we of course find it unfamiliar. By walking around for a while, however, looking into various rooms and peering into cupboards, we quickly get to know it. But what if we cannot enter the house, and our only knowledge of it comes from the instructions and plans that were used to build it? Moreover, what if those instructions and plans are written in a highly technical language that we find intimidating and incomprehensible? What if, try as we may, we cannot form any mental picture of the house? Then we are not going to get much of a sense of what it is like to live there. We are not going to be able to enter the house even in our imagination.

—Keith Devlin, *The Math Gene*

The Country Called School

Learning is natural; schooling is not. Schools are countries to which we send our children, expecting these places and the people who work there to help draw out and shape our children into the successful adults we want them to become. As with travel to other countries, however, people truly benefit from the time spent there only to the extent that they can and do participate. If someone doesn't know the language, the customs, the culture—well, that person will feel like the outsider they are. As Gerald Graff, author of *Clueless in Academe* (2003) puts it, "schooling takes students who are perfectly street-smart and exposes them to the life of the mind in ways that make them feel dumb" (2).

This is precisely how I felt when I arrived at college. I lacked any understanding of the language. The culture of academics confused me. The conventions that governed students' behaviors and habits were invisible to me. Those who thrived in school seemed to have been born into the culture, to have heard the language all their life, and to know inherently what mattered, what was worth paying attention to, how much effort was appropriate. Teachers somehow seemed to expect that we all came equipped with the same luggage, all of which contained the necessary tools and strategies that would ensure our success in their classes and, ultimately, school. It wasn't so.

When I entered the Peace Corps several years later, the first thing they did was prepare us for all that we would face. They provided this cultural training for a very simple reason: to ensure our—and thus, their—success once we began our work "in country." They took us to Harper's Ferry, West Virginia, where we participated in simulations and assessed our performance, which was then examined by Tunisian RPCVs (returned Peace Corps volunteers) who had already been successful in the environment and work situations we were preparing to enter. During this same time, we learned about Tunisia, its ways, its history, and its culture, all of which were heavily influenced by Islam. By the time we walked off the plane in Tunisia, we had a context for whatever we encountered on the streets and at work. While we knew plenty about the culture, however, we knew nothing about the language; indeed, it was as foreign as a language could possibly be.

Instead of running right into the classroom to begin teaching for two years, we settled in and began to study the language. Not only was the language utterly new to us, but so were the customs of the classroom and the methods of instruction. Intelligent men and women, sometimes more than twice the age of our teachers, were occasionally reduced to tears as they struggled to meet the challenges of learning the Arabic language. But that feeling of belonging, of making a home for ourselves in the midst of what first felt so strange to us— that feeling was slow to come for most of us, and purchased with long hours of hard learning. Those who had learned other languages excelled because they knew how to learn a language; they were strategic learners who were further bolstered by the confidence that this was a challenge they had already met. Among this group, the most able learner was Paul Bell, a young man whose parents had lived in Tunisia until Paul was six; his nanny had spoken to him in not just Arabic but *Tunisian* Arabic. Not surprisingly, Paul learned it fastest and spoke it best. On the other end of the continuum were those for whom the language did not come easily at all. While there are different possible explanations for their struggles to learn the language, it is useful to consider their cognitive overload in the context of several constraints (Olson 2002) that affect people's performance in more than just the academic domain:

Cognitive constraints. Students can be constrained by the knowledge they have to bring to the task—especially if that knowledge is limited. To lessen the cognitive constraints, the teacher must scaffold activities that help students tap and mobilize existing knowledge as well as construct new knowledge.

Linguistic constraints. Students may not possess the language adequate to understand or produce text. To lessen these constraints, the teacher must design activities that create a language-rich environment for students to draw and build upon.

Communicative constraints. Students are often constrained by the audience for whom they perceive they are reading or writing—which is, in most cases, the teacher. To reduce these constraints, the teacher can broaden the audiences students write to and for, downplay his or her role as assessor, enlist students as peer responders to give and receive feedback on each other's texts, and foster more self-monitoring and self-reflection on the part of the students.

Contextual constraints. Contextual constraints involve the circumstances or context in which reading and writing take place. If students are to produce multiple-draft readings and writings, the teacher must adopt a "less is more" philosophy and allow for the extended time necessary for ideas to evolve. Further, rather than focusing exclusively on the finished product, the teacher should value all of the facets of the composing process.

Textual constraints. Students bring to the mental or written texts they are composing the influence of the content and the form of all the prior texts they have read or written. These texts can powerfully influence the student's composing process. An experienced, well-practiced student will have a wide array of options to choose from, whereas a less experienced student will work from a limited range of resources. To lessen textual constraints, the teacher should expose students to a rich array of models to enrich their textual repertoire. (Adapted from Frederiksen and Dominic, 1981, pp. 17–20.)

Affective constraints. Researchers tend to zero in on the cognitive constraints that readers and writers must deal with when they compose but the affective constraints students face when they do not find school reading and writing tasks to be meaningful can loom just as large. Indeed, lacking the confidence, the willingness, or the motivation to undertake a challenging reading or writing task can be as debilitating as lacking the capacity to do so. To lessen these constraints, teachers must actively seek to make reading and writing instruction meaningful by building in as many concrete, personal, and interactive activities as possible and by helping to make the texts their students read and write accessible, relevant, and engaging. (21)

What does all this have to do with school, with academic literacy? Everything, I would argue. School *is* a country, a place where some come with a native's understanding of how things work. Mike Rose, author of *Lives on the Boundary*, analyzed college-level instructional tasks over the course of a year to identify what students were expected to know and be able to do. Rose's investigation of the educational terrain yielded six essential academic skills that allow a student to navigate their way through the landscape ahead: defining, summarizing, serializing, classifying, comparing, and analyzing (1989, xiii). Other recent books focusing on academic literacy emphasize the importance of "argument literacy" (Graff 2003, 3) and "essayist literacy" (Brandt 2001, 56) as intellectual passports that grant students access to "the culture of ideas and arguments," the "academic club," which demands that each person arrive with a fully developed "ability to listen, summarize, and respond," all of which amounts to being "educated" (Graff 2003, 3) and thus a member of the "literacy club" (Smith 1988). Still others (Schoenbach et al. 1999; DeStigter 2001; Zmuda and Tomaino 2001; Brandt 2001; and Freedman 2000) have found that many students with obvious talent arrive at school lacking the academic knowledge, skills, and abilities needed to succeed there. Schoenbach et al. encountered this phenomenon at Thurgood Marshall Academic High School in San Francisco: "Students were told before entering . . . that the word *academic* in the school's name meant they would be expected to work hard. . . . Many of them were unprepared for the demands of a curriculum geared to prepare them to succeed at a four-year college. . . . A high number of . . . students were having difficulty getting through heavy reading requirements that [the] curriculum demanded" (1999, 46). Only when teachers accept responsibility for teaching students these skills can those teachers expect students to feel at home and succeed in their academic classes. As one Thurgood Marshall student said, "Since I've been in this [academic literacy] class and you've been stressing reading, it's become a custom to me . . . now when I go out I take my SSR book most of the time instead of my Walkman" (45).

Academic Demands

In recent years, several important reports and programs have emerged, all of which look not only at reading but the school skills needed to succeed in secondary and higher education. In a joint report, for example, the California Academic

Senates—representing the community colleges, state colleges, and universities—identified the following core academic "habits of mind" needed to succeed at the postsecondary level, though one can easily see their relevance to elementary, middle, and high school as well:

BROAD INTELLECTUAL PRACTICES

- Exhibit curiosity
- Experiment with new ideas
- See other points of view
- Challenge their own beliefs
- Engage in intellectual discussions
- Ask provocative questions
- Generate hypotheses
- Exhibit respect for other viewpoints
- Read with awareness of self and others

CLASSROOM BEHAVIORS

- Ask questions for clarification
- Be attentive in class
- Come to class prepared
- Complete assignments on time
- Contribute to class discussions

ADDITIONAL COLLEGE EXPECTATIONS

- Respect facts and information in situations where feelings and intuitions often prevail
- Be aware that rhetorics of argumentation and interrogation are calibrated to disciplines, purposes, and audiences
- Embrace the value of research to explore new ideas through reading and writing
- Develop a capacity to work hard and to expect high standards
- Show initiative and develop ownership of their education (Intersegmental Committee of Academic Senates 2002; *note:* the complete text of the Executive Summary is available in Appendix B)

This list of habits illustrates the complex array of competencies students must develop and learn to use flexibly in different academic contexts. For those raised in academic families, where many of these same values—promptness, organization, empathy, intellectual discipline, discussion—weave themselves into family conversations and interactions for twelve years, the increased academic demands of the middle school and, subsequently, high school feel much like home. On the other hand, those students who arrive from distant countries where circumstances such as war prevented them from attending school at all find school a confusing, disorienting place. And one certainly need not come from a different country to feel this same disorientation in the academic culture of a typical high school. Anthropologist Clifford Geertz (1973), writing about this feeling of disorientation, says: "We learn this when we come into a strange country with entirely different traditions; and, what is more, even given the mastery of the country's language. We do not *understand* the people. (And not because of not knowing what they are saying to themselves.) We cannot find our feet with them" (13).

Biblical scholar Walter Breuggemann (1995), studying the psalms, noticed a three-part cycle that Geertz's comment brings to mind. Breuggeman sees the psalms as describing three phases: orientation, disorientation, and new orientation. When Geertz speaks of being unable to "find our feet," he refers to the feeling of disorientation we all experience when we enter into a new environment. If you want to know what disorientation looks and feels like, follow a new middle or high school student around on the first day of school. The important question is, What can be done to move these students from disorientation to a new orientation that will allow them to succeed in the new environment? And to make matters more difficult, we should realize that a challenging teacher will ask students to move through that cycle repeatedly throughout the year, for as students master one task or idea, they should, if they are challenged and supported, move up to the next level of complexity, which will give them another taste of that disorientation. The difference between successful and unsuccessful students? Successful students not only learn how to move through that cycle by employing various strategies but learn that they *can* transcend their feelings of disorientation and move toward a feeling of new orientation.

Demystifying School Success

Geertz's remarks raise another angle on the issue of students' acclimation to academic culture: teachers' perspectives toward these neophytes. For decades, students who could not find their feet in academic settings were ignored, dismissed as just not cut out for such work. Many teachers absolved themselves of responsibility for the students, their well-being, and their intellectual development. The standards movement of the last decade has directly challenged that, has said, in essence, the teacher's job is to teach these students not only to survive but to thrive in academic settings and demonstrate all that knowledge on the intellectual equivalent of a citizenship test: a high school exit exam. Todd DeStigter (2001), who followed "the forgotten students of Addison High" (i.e., Latino students at a Midwest suburban high school where the vast majority was white), asked faculty and counselors to determine the "top indicators of college failure." Teachers identified the following:

- Weak study and critical thinking skills
- Poor time management
- Ineffective reading, writing, and math skills
- An inability to apply effective test-taking strategies
- Weak communication skills and need to define their educational priorities
- Lack of high school preparation that addresses conflict management/ resolution
- An inability to accept diversity
- Inappropriately used drugs and alcohol
- Lack of access to necessary supplies (i.e., calculator, computer) and insufficient funds to access higher education
- Entered the employment cycle (which is necessary for survival) and thereby experienced further hindrance and interference to academic success (82)

Analyzing these responses, DeStigter found that most of them focus on what the teachers perceive to be "defects" in the students' intellect or character, which suggests that the faculty, when trying to explain students' failure, "were looking not at themselves and their school, but at the students' upbringing" (82). Lisa Delpit's (1995) study of "other people's children" argues that schools are governed by "the culture of power," something others (Friere 1993; Brown 1993; Meier 2001; Pope 2001; Cushman 2003) emphasize in their own writings. Delpit identifies five aspects of power that influence students' experience of and performance within the academic environment:

1. Issues of power are enacted in classrooms.
2. There are codes or rules for participating in power; that is, there is a "culture of power."
3. The rules of the culture of power are a reflection of the rules of the culture of those who have power.

4. If you are not already a participant in the culture of power, being told explicitly the rules of that culture makes acquiring power easier.
5. Those with power are frequently least aware of—or least willing to acknowledge—its existence. Those with less power are often most aware of its existence. (1995, 25)

Recently, numerous programs and methods have emerged to help students acquire this power that Delpit speaks of and others allude to in their own writings. Only by demystifying (Levine 2002; 2003) such social and cognitive processes can those without power begin to gain it; the same argument for economic power, or "financial intelligence," runs throughout the popular *Rich Dad* series (Kiyosaki 1997), in which the author argues that rich people ensure their kids' financial success by teaching them (i.e., demystifying) how money and the financial world work. One of the most successful academic literacy programs, AVID (Advancement via Individual Determination), uses a set of carefully refined methods to demystify academic success, one of which is a highly structured binder:

> Binder checks had multiple purposes: to teach kids how to organize the chaos of their studies (and minds) into a coherent order, to see when their assignments were due, to plan their time, to find their notes and papers, and to make them take responsibility for their schoolwork. . . . These habits of mind were fundamental to organizing the daily tasks of school. . . . But many of the kids were ignorant of how the education system worked. Education was not a tradition in their families and they were doomed to fail, not because they were dumb, but because they did not know simple things like when assignments were due, how to budget time, or when to ask for help. Children of college graduates were usually taught this at home. It seemed simple: By learning the rudimentary skills, habits, and disciplines, AVID students would gain freedom to use their minds, to shape time to their needs—to soar. (Freedman 2000, 72)

What distinguishes AVID (and explains its students' remarkable achievements) is that it teaches the whole student, does for them what the various Peace Corps trainings did for me to help me find a home within a culture that was so different from my own, and develop the skills and knowledge I needed to succeed once in that environment. The AVID program, through its methods and the community that emerges within its classes, gives students those keys to the kingdom that Lisa Delpit refers to and Mike Rose (1989) describes when he observes students struggling in school:

> Every day in our schools and colleges, young people confront reading and writing tasks that seem hard or unusual, that confuse them, that they fail. But if you can get close enough to their failure, you'll find knowledge that the

assignment didn't tap, ineffective rules and strategies that have a logic of their own; you'll find clues, as well, to the complex ties between literacy and culture, to the tremendous difficulties our children face as they attempt to find their places in the American educational system. Some, like Laura, are struck dumb by the fear of making a mistake; others, like Bobby, feel estranged because familiar cognitive landscapes have shifted, because once-effective strategies have been rendered obsolete; and still others are like the young men and women in Dr. Gunner's classroom: They know more than their tests reveal but haven't been taught how to weave that knowledge into coherent patterns. For Laura, Bobby, and the others the pronouncement of deficiency came late, but for many it comes as early as the first grade. Kids find themselves sitting on the threatening boundaries of the classroom. Marginal. Designated as "slow learners" or "remedial" or, eventually, "vocational." (8)

Referring back to my own school experience, one incident comes to mind when I think about Rose's passage. After *barely* graduating, I enrolled in a community college the next fall. Entering students had to take placement exams. Arriving at my English class the first day, I learned that I had received a very high score on the writing placement test and was put in an advanced-level writing class. This dumbfounded me, but what I remember most is what happened several days later. Feeling all pumped up with this new knowledge about my abilities (Honors!—well of course, why not?), I sat down to write my first paper. The day after I turned it in (I even typed it!), the professor said there was obviously a mistake, for my work on the paper was substandard, hardly worthy of someone who scored at the honors level on the placement exam. I didn't question his judgment for a minute; after all, had I been so "smart" I surely would have done better in school. I lacked faith in my own mind and abilities and readily deferred to those in this new country (called College) who told me where to go and what to do (or not to do). This professor was the academic equivalent of a customs agent, like the one years later in Korea who told me I did not have the requisite papers to enter Japan and would therefore have to stay in Korea until I got my papers in order. So I transferred to a "more appropriate" English class to begin the process of learning the language and customs required by college professors.

Pursuing and Experiencing Academic Success

What does my college experience look like at the high school level? Here's what Christian Segarini, a freshman with some learning difficulties and honors-level skateboarding skills, wrote at the end of his first year of high school:

> One thing I learned this hole year was that school was so easy the first week but when the second week came the homework started to be handed out and

the class work got hard. Suddenly I didn't think school was that easy any more. The weeks past and I was doing pretty good in some of my classes. When I got my first progress report it was exhalent but when my second progress report came out my grades weren't as good as they where before.

So I decided to try better in school because it was harder than I thought it would be. I tried really hard in school and began to raise my grades. When the third progress report cam out, I began to do better and raise my grades more. So after the progress report came out we had finals coming up in a couple of weeks. I began to study more and try to finish all homework assignments and projects. I was doing pretty good on the homework and the projects but I wasn't doing so well on my test for Math and History. So I decided I need to go to tutoring for math and study more for the history test.

After a few weeks we had a test in math and in History. I tried my best on both and I got a C on both of them. I was so proud of my self. Finally the last week came for finals. The first final I took was in P.E. and that was pretty easy. I got an A– on that. The second final was pretty easy too. I got a B+ on that and the third final I did pretty good to. Finally the last 3 classes where up. They where pretty hard for me. It was math and I didn't do so good on that. I got a D+ and English class was next I got a C+ in that then finally History came I got a D+ in that. I noticed that I need to study more and that school is harder than you think it is. For me it was hard.

Compare Christian's experiences with the one Andrea Glick describes in this excerpt from her graduation speech:

During these four years, we had to make many choices, including which high school we would attend. As all the families can see, each one of tonight's graduates chose the right school and is sitting on this stage as proof of his/her accomplishments. This choice began the long journey.

As freshmen, it was now time to register for classes and decide what we wanted to take. Some students knew exactly what they wanted to do and where they were heading. Others just wanted to take the required classes to graduate. Then, there was the choice of which organizations or athletic teams to join. Soccer? Drama? Student government? Some students were involved in as many activities as could fit their schedule. Along with these decisions, our choice of friends was a major factor in determining whether high school was a positive or negative experience. As time went on, we began to know who our friends were. We were trying to find a niche in a school with more than 1,300 students.

Then, sophomore year began. It was a minor transition because there were still two more years of high school left. Some of us began looking at colleges and trying to pick college-level classes, and others were just laying low trying to get a passing grade. Either way, our third year of high school was right around the corner.

Junior year brought on an entirely different set of choices. Will we still have time to participate in school activities? Do we want to go to a big or small college, public or private? These were difficult decisions. That was why we had our counselors, teachers, and parents to look to for guidance in helping us make some of these decisions.

As our junior year came to an end, many of us were anxious to become seniors. When it was time to choose classes, we initially thought an easy schedule would be the way to go. Unfortunately, colleges still looked at our senior year. The common thought of "senior year is the easiest year of high school" soon became a misconception. Many of us enrolled in advanced placement courses to appeal to the best schools in the country. Those of us in other classes worked hard as well. So our final year in high school started, and we began filling out college applications. When these were completed, the acceptances and, in some cases, rejections began pouring in. This was why we had worked so hard the past four years, and now colleges were acknowledging our accomplishments. The choice of a college was tough, but once we made it, we were smiling because we knew we were going to have a future.

Now we are here tonight. We will be able to decide for ourselves what will make us happy and fulfill our dreams. So I say to the graduating class of 2003, embrace this opportunity, make the right choices, and go out into the world with the knowledge that you CAN succeed.

It's easy to read Andrea's speech and assume she is guaranteed success at the university level. And Andrea is. Her father is a lead administrator at a local college; her mother is an educational leader at the same high school Andrea attended. Her parents not only encourage and support Andrea's many choices, but provide constant models of how to explain, analyze, evaluate, problem solve, and persuade. School, and eventually the university, feels like an additional room attached to her house.

My concerns, however, are not limited to struggling students. Of all the kids who will enter college in the fall with Andrea—kids who performed very well in high school—roughly 40 percent will not be prepared to meet the academic demands of their courses. According to *Academic Literacies: A Statement of Competencies*:

- Eight-three percent of the faculty say that the lack of analytical reading skills contributes to students' lack of success in a course.
- Only one third of entering college students are sufficiently prepared for the two most frequently assigned writing tasks: analyzing information or arguments and synthesizing information from several sources. (Intersegmental Committee of Academic Senates 2002)

A separate study conducted by Public Agenda (1999) summed up its key findings in the graph shown in Figure 1.1.

Understanding University Success, another recent study, defines academic success as "the ability to do well enough in college entry-level core academic courses to meet general education requirements and to continue on to major in a particular area" (Conley 2003, 9). The report also identifies key "habits of mind" that help students succeed in academic courses:

- Critical thinking
- Analytical thinking and problem solving
- An inquisitive nature and interest in taking advantage of what a research university has to offer

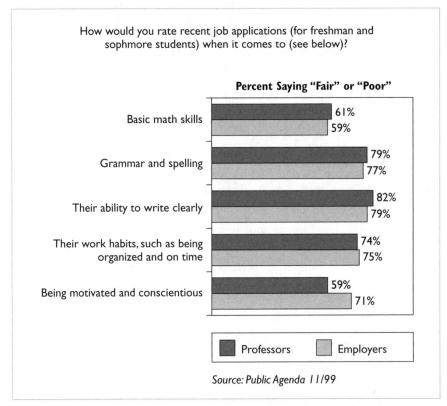

How would you rate recent job applications (for freshman and sophmore students) when it comes to (see below)?

Percent Saying "Fair" or "Poor"

Basic math skills — Professors 61% / Employers 59%

Grammar and spelling — Professors 79% / Employers 77%

Their ability to write clearly — Professors 82% / Employers 79%

Their work habits, such as being organized and on time — Professors 74% / Employers 75%

Being motivated and conscientious — Professors 59% / Employers 71%

■ Professors ■ Employers

Source: Public Agenda 11/99

FIGURE 1.1. Public Agenda 1999. This graph shows how professors and employers responded to the question shown at the top of the chart.

- The willingness to accept critical feedback and to adjust based on such feedback
- Openness to possible failures from time to time
- The ability and desire to cope with frustrating and ambiguous learning tasks
- The ability to express one's self in writing and orally in clear and convincing fashion
- To discern the relative importance and credibility of various sources of information
- To draw inferences and reach conclusions independently
- To use technology as a tool to assist the learning process rather than as a crutch (8)

Evolving Notions of Literacy

While these statistics about students' performance are not new, the current response to them is. Books like *Reading for Understanding* (Schoenbach et al. 1999) and *The Reader's Handbook* (Burke 2002) represent important new trends in education; they articulate what effective students do when they read, write, study, and take tests. Ineffective and unsuccessful students may well think there is such a thing as the school gene, which they simply did not inherit; as *The Reader's Handbook* explains, however:

> There are two kinds of readers: active readers and passive readers. Passive readers let a writer's words wash over them without giving much thought to what the words mean. As a result, passive readers can find themselves drowning in a sea of words. Active readers, on the other hand, take control of what they're reading—from the very fist page. They think about what a writer has to say, and at the same time they think about their own responses to the reading. Active reading means asking questions, agreeing and disagreeing, and applying what you've learned from reading to your own life. An active reader interacts with the writer. (49)

As simple as these active strategies seem, they never occurred to me; I had no idea what effective readers (or writers, or students, or test takers) did. This process of looking at what effective people do began in earnest back in the eighties, when then-President Reagan's secretary of labor investigated workplace standards and expectations. The result was the *SCANS* (*Secretary of Labor's Commission on Achieving Necessary Skills*) *Report.* Central to that report were the "competencies" identified by employers in all fields as essential to success:

BASIC SKILLS: Reads, writes, performs arithmetic and mathematical operations, listens and speaks

1. *Reading:* Locates, understands, and interprets written information in prose and in documents such as manuals, graphs, and schedules.
2. *Writing:* Communicates thoughts, ideas, information, and messages in writing, and creates documents such as letters, directions, manuals, reports, graphs, and flow charts.
3. *Arithmetic:* Performs basic computations; uses basic numerical concepts such as whole numbers, etc.
4. *Mathematics:* Approaches practical problems by choosing appropriately from a variety of mathematical techniques.
5. *Listening:* Receives, attends to, interprets, and responds to verbal messages and other cues.
6. *Speaking:* Organizes ideas and communicates orally.

THINKING SKILLS: Thinks creatively, makes decisions, solves problems, visualizes, and knows how to learn and reason

1. *Creative thinking:* Generates new ideas.
2. *Decision-making:* Specifies goals and constraints, generates alternatives, considers risks, and evaluates and chooses best alternative.
3. *Problem solving:* Recognizes problems and devises and implements plan of action.
4. *Seeing things in the mind's eye:* Organizes and processes symbols, pictures, graphs, objects, and other information.
5. *Knowing how to learn:* Uses efficient learning techniques to acquire and apply new knowledge and skills.
6. *Reasoning:* Discovers a rule or principle underlying the relationship between two or more objects and applies it when solving a problem.

PERSONAL QUALITIES: Displays responsibility, self-esteem, sociability, self-management, integrity, and honesty

1. *Responsibility:* Exerts a high level of effort and perseveres towards goal attainment.
2. *Self-esteem:* Believes in own self-worth and maintains a positive view of self.

3. *Sociability:* Demonstrates understanding, friendliness, adaptability, empathy, and politeness in group settings.
4. *Self-management:* Assesses self accurately, sets personal goals, monitors progress, and exhibits self-control.
5. *Integrity/honesty:* Chooses ethical courses of action. (U.S. Department of Labor 1991)

The country has begun to pay attention, to realize that we have no reason to expect success or improvement in areas where students lack essential competencies, capacities, and content knowledge. Several programs show promise: Talent Development High School at Johns Hopkins University, Mary Catherine Swanson's AVID, Robert Moses' Algebra Project, the Strategic Literacy Initiative's Reading Apprenticeship, the Puente Project, and my own evolving program, ACCESS. A number of reports (Conley 2003; Intersegmental Committee of Academic Senates 2002), books (Light 2001; Pope 2001; Rose 1989; Mooney and Cole 2000; Hrabowski, Maton, and Greif 1998; DeStigter 2001; Fielding, Schoenbach, and Jordan 2003; Freedman 2000; Boiarsky 2003), articles (Klemp 2003) have begun to focus on what is coming to be known as academic literacy. Synthesizing many of these ideas (from multiple sources), Ron Klemp, in an article titled "Academic Literacy: Making Students Content Area Learners" (2003), focuses on "students' ability to successfully negotiate the demands of texts used in classrooms across every district in the United States" (1). Klemp goes on to define academic literacy, saying that "becoming academically literate means that a learner has an inventory of effective strategies to meet the demands of different forms of text" (1). Klemp cites a joint publication by the Northwest Regional Educational Laboratory, the National Council of Teachers of English, and the International Reading Association, which distinguishes between three levels of literacy:

Basic literacy refers to the ability to decode, recognize, and comprehend printed signs, symbols, and words.

Proficient literacy refers to the ability to extend ideas, make inferences, draw conclusions, and make connections to personal experiences from printed texts.

Advanced literacy refers to the ability to use language to solve problems and to extend cognitive development. New understandings within and across texts and the ability to summarize, evaluate, and apply strategies to texts to construct meaning from various perspectives also describes someone at an advanced level of literacy.

The problem—or rather, the challenge—is that literacy is not static, but evolving. "Literacy needs to be understood in terms of time and place and people, communication systems, and technologies and values—and these are always changing" (Langer 2003, 3). Langer goes on to say that "as we become more of a technological and communication society, literacy demands become more specialized and more complex—issues of language and literacy gain prominence, and the need for a literate mind becomes more essential" (4). Others (Brandt 2001; Gilster 1997; Burke 2001; Myers 1996) reiterate this notion of literacy as a set of skills, capacities that are evolving at ever-increasing rates, leaving those who have learned the last set of cognitive skills in the wake of those who have embraced and learned the new set of literacies. Literacy is not, then, a grab bag of skills one learns once and for all; instead, it requires developing what Langer (2003) calls a "literate mind," by which she means:

> . . . being literate as the ability to behave like a literate person—to engage in the kinds of thinking and reasoning people generally use when they read and write, even in situations where reading and writing are not involved (such as inspecting and analyzing meanings from a variety of vantage points with or without texts—like a movie or play; the mental act itself is a literate act). I call this ability "literate thinking." (5)

It is this mind that will be ready to live and succeed in the increasingly global economy, where the manual skills of the past continue to give way to the more mental, service-oriented skills of the future. What are these skills, these workplace literacies? The following adaptation of the SCANS findings, which were created by a group of community and business leaders, offers a useful summary:

INFORMATION PROCESSING
- Select and evaluate information
- Select ways to organize information
- Interpret and communicate information

COMPUTER USAGE
- Use word processing, communication
- Use a graphic program, multimedia
- Use a spreadsheet program, database

TECHNOLOGY USAGE
- Set up appropriate machines and equipment
- Produce a product using technology
- Maintain and troubleshoot technology

RESOURCING

- Schedule time to meet task or project deadlines
- Select appropriate human and material resources
- Allocate resources to complete a task or project

ORAL COMMUNICATION

- Deliver messages with clarity
- Follow oral directions
- Participate in group discussions

READING

- Investigate meaning of unknown words
- Extract the main ideas of messages
- Identify relevant details, facts, and specification from reading

MATHEMATICS USAGE

- Use measuring tools and systems
- Use basic computational skills
- Use graphic formats to display or obtain information

SYSTEM USAGE

- Identify the system and its purpose
- Monitor and improve performance
- Adapt to situational changes

LEADERSHIP

- Organize group work
- Involve all group members
- Set positive examples for others

GROUP DYNAMICS

- Contribute ideas, suggestions, and effort for completion of group tasks
- Solve conflicts in positive ways
- Cooperate as a member of a multi-ethnic, mixed-gender team

PROBLEM SOLVING

- Identify and define problems or issues
- Generate and select from alternative strategies to solve problems
- Consider consequences of actions
- Make informed decisions

RESPONSIBILITY
- Display punctuali...
- Meet deadlines a...
- Take care of mat...

SELF-CONFIDENCE
- Display confid...
- Demonstrate i...
- Assess and ev...

SELF-MANAGEM...
- Exhibit self...
- Work with...
- Evaluate a...

INTEGRITY
- Exhibit i...
- Respect rights and prope...

SOCIABILITY
- Compromise
- Exhibit sensitivity to the attitudes, values, and feelings of others

PERSONAL IDENTIFICATION
- Produce a portfolio
- Produce a resume

Teaching Academic Success

Can we *teach* students to be academically successful? Lampert, in a chapter titled "Teaching Students to Be People Who Study in School" (2001), argues we can and must teach students to have the skills and disposition needed to *be* students. She says, "Teachers can also be said to 'make' or 'construct' *students* into resources that can be used to promote learning by teaching them to be the kinds of people who study in the classroom and who expect others to do so as well" (265). Along with Lampert, I believe we can teach students to be successful students, but first we must clarify what we mean by success. Between GPAs, various state and national exams, SATs, ACTs, AP exams, and the extent to which a student takes challenging courses, we have many numbers to use. In our competitive society, only the highest counts; as a parent snapped to one of my colleagues last year during a conference in which she was arguing that her daughter should receive an A because she did so well on the final exam, "A B+ is *useless.*" But are good grades even a genuine measure of academic success? In *"Doing School,"* Denise Clark Pope (2001) uncovered a darker side to such academic success:

> To keep up her grades, Eve sleeps just two to three hours each night and lives in a constant state of stress. Kevin faces anxiety and frustration as he attempts to balance the high expectations of his father with his own desire to "have a life" outside of school. Michelle struggles to find a way to pursue her love for drama without compromising her college prospects. And both Teresa and Roberto resort to drastic actions when they worry that they will not maintain the grades they need for future careers. All of them admit to doing things that they're not proud of in order to succeed in school. These students explain that they are busy at what they call "doing school." They realize they are caught in a system where achievement depends more on "doing"—going through the correct motions—than on learning and engaging with the curriculum. Instead of thinking deeply about the content of their courses and delving into projects and assignments, the students focus on managing the work load and honing strategies that will help them to achieve high grades. (4)

Of course it is not the student who straddles the B+/A− border that concerns us; rather, we worry about the disengaged, the disaffected, wondering what we can do to help them succeed both in school and in life. Programs like AVID, the Algebra Project, and Johns Hopkins University's Talent Development High School Program show that such success is possible. Essential to such progress is improved articulation between students and teachers about what students must know in order to succeed in academic classes; moreover, teachers must accept responsibility for teaching students these skills, developing the requisite capacities needed to succeed. Robert Marzano (2001) revisited Bloom's taxonomy (1956) to see if it reflected the kind of teaching and learning his research (Marzano et al. 2001) found to most effective. Concluding that Bloom et al. had not offered a complete or accurate picture of educational objectives, Marzano offered his own New Taxonomy of Educational Objectives (2001), the key principles of which are included in Figure 1.2.

It is easy to look at Marzano's objectives in the light of the past and say, as many teachers did, that most kids cannot perform above Level 1. When students like Andrea or those in most honors classes arrive at high school prepared to get down to work right away, we too often think that is the standard, that students should come to school knowing all they need to know to be able to do what we ask, so that we can teach content and not skills. A second look

OBJECTIVES FOR THE LEVELS OF MARZANO'S NEW TAXONOMY

	DESCRIPTION
Level 6: Self-System Examining Importance Examining Efficacy Examining Emotional Response Examining Motivation	**Beliefs and goals used to make judgments about engaging in a new task.** • Identifies how important the knowledge is and reasoning underlying this perception. • Identifies beliefs about ability to improve ability or understanding related to knowledge. • Identifies emotional responses to knowledge and reasons for these responses. • Identifies own level of motivation to improve competence or understanding.
Level 5: Metacognition Goal Specification Process Monitoring Monitoring Clarity Monitoring Accuracy	**Sets goals relative to new task; designs strategies to accomplish this goal.** • Sets a plan for goals relative to the knowledge. • Monitors the execution of knowledge. • Determines the extent to which he/she has clarity about the knowledge. • Determines the extent to which he/she is accurate about the knowledge.
Level 4: Utilization Decision Making Problem Solving Experimental Inquiry Investigation	**Processes someone uses to accomplish a specific task.** • Uses the knowledge to make decisions or makes decisions about the use of knowledge. • Uses the knowledge to solve problems or solves problems about the knowledge. • Uses the knowledge to generate and test hypotheses or generates and tests hypotheses about the knowledge. • Uses the knowledge to conduct investigations or conducts investigations about the knowledge.
Level 3: Analysis Matching Classifying Error Analysis Generalizing Specifying	**Involves the generation of new information not already possessed by individual.** • Identifies important similarities and differences between knowledge. • Identifies superordinate and subordinate categories related to knowledge. • Identifies errors in presentation or use of knowledge. • Constructs new generalizations or principles based on knowledge. • Identifies specific applications or logical consequences of knowledge.
Level 2: Comprehension Synthesis Representation	**Translates knowledge into a form appropriate for storage in permanent memory.** • Identifies the basic structure of knowledge and the critical as opposed to noncritical characteristics. • Accurately represents in nonlinguistic or symbolic form the basic structure of knowledge and the critical as opposed to noncritical aspects.
Level 1: Retrieval Recall Execution	**The activation and transfer of knowledge from permanent to working memory.** • Can identify or recognize features of info but does not necessarily understand the structure of knowledge or can differentiate critical from noncritical components. • Can perform a procedure without significant error but does not necessarily understand how and why the procedure works.

FIGURE 1.2. For a more complete description of this taxonomy, see Marzano's book *Designing a New Taxonomy of Educational Objectives*. © Marzano 2001. Formatted by Jim Burke.

at Marzano's taxonomy, however, illustrates the range of skills required of students; such skills are often neither intuitive nor familiar to students, as Pope (2001) shows:

> Often when a student like Berto does not act in accordance with the majority of students, teachers are caught off guard. They usually don't have the time to cater to an individual student's needs, and they have come to expect and perhaps rely on the more typical, less diligent behavior. If Berto, as he believes, studies as hard as his "smart" friends, he may not achieve their high grades, in part because he does not completely understand the system in which he is acting. Schools are set up, with their tight time schedules and overcrowded classrooms, to demand certain behaviors from students, and Berto has not yet figured out how to behave in a way that meets his own standards for excellence as well as those of his teachers. (135)

When taught these skills, students regularly perform at or near the expected levels so long as they learn not only to do the work but those strategies that will allow them to solve similar and progressively difficult problems within that domain (Tomlinson 1999; Stigler and Hiebert 1999).

The Academic Literacy Evaluation (Figure 1.3) reflects my attempt to articulate what successful students do. The SCANS report had tried to do this for the workplace, asking what people who were effective and successful knew and were able to do. The Academic Literacy Evaluation clearly demonstrates that success in academic settings and on academic tasks involves much more than the obvious skills of reading, writing, and 'rithmetic. I am reminded of the time I tried to help a pitcher on my son's little league team by breaking down where his pitching motion was going astray; no matter how I tried to explain it, I kept realizing how many operations were happening simultaneously. The next week, however, another coach visited, one with an expertise in pitching who was able to not only analyze the pitcher's motion but articulate the problem in language (and with demonstrations) that was clear and made a difference. Such modeling by a master (which all teachers are within their discipline) achieved the outcome I could not; as Schoenbach et al. (1999) write, "in a reading apprenticeship, teachers invite students to become partners . . . to become better readers by making the teacher's reading process visible to them, by helping them gain insight into their own reading processes, and by having them learn a repertoire of cognitive problem-solving strategies" (14). They go on to conclude, "A reading apprenticeship is at heart a partnership of expertise, drawing both on what subject area teachers know and do as disciplinary readers and on adolescents' unique and often underestimated strengths as learners" (14).

ACADEMIC LITERACY EVALUATION		
1 = Never 2 = Rarely 3 = Sometimes 4 = Usually 5 = Always B = Before A = After the specified period of time		
B	**A**	**Basic Skills: Reads, writes, performs arithmetic and mathematical operations, listens, and speaks**
		1. I read actively, using a variety of strategies and asking questions to help me understand what I read.
		2. I identify the main idea and supporting details in informational texts.
		3. I use computers to write, research, and/or present.
		4. I follow oral directions, using strategies to remember and/or comprehend them.
B	**A**	**Thinking Skills: Thinks creatively, makes decisions, solves problems, visualizes, and knows how to learn and reason**
		5. I use strategies to help me do well on quizzes and tests.
		6. I use different strategies and techniques to help me remember information.
		7. I use a reading process to help me understand what I read.
		8. I use a variety of notetaking strategies to help me read, write, learn, and think.
		9. I consider what I learn from different perspectives to help me better understand it.
		10. I connect what I study now with what I know from experience and have learned in school.
		11. I know how I learn best and take advantage of this knowledge.
		12. I monitor my reading so I know how well I understand the text and which strategies to use.
		13. I preread all texts before I read the entire text and do the assignment.
		14. I use strategies to determine the quality and importance of information.
		15. I set a purpose before I read, write, speak, listen, design, or think.
		16. I formulate an argument/thesis and support it with details, examples, and quotations.
		17. I read the directions so I know what to do, how to do it, and the order in which things should be done.
		18. I use a variety of strategies to help me visualize what I read/learn.
		19. I use strategies to help me generate ideas when writing, reading, designing, planning, or thinking.
		20. I prepare myself to read, write, listen, watch, or learn.
		21. I find out the criteria by which my work will be graded before I begin.
		22. I learn from my errors, mistakes, and experiences.
		23. I consult other students for suggestions about how to succeed in a class or on an assignment.

FIGURE 1.3. Academic Literacy Evaluation. Students complete this self-evaluation at the beginning of the first semester and end of the second semester as part of their reflection on academic improvement. From *The Teacher's Daybook* (© Burke 2001).

B	A		
		24.	I tell my teachers what helps me learn and succeed.
		25.	I prioritize my work according to time, difficulty, urgency, and resources needed.
		26.	I dedicate a specific time for school work each day.
		27.	I study in a place that has no distractions and those materials I need.
B	**A**		**Personal Qualities: Displays responsibility, self-esteem, sociability, self-management, integrity, and honesty**
		28.	I write down all homework assignments in a planner or on a dedicated page in a binder.
		29.	I keep track of my standing in each class.
		30.	I bring my book and other materials to class every day.
		31.	I have my Internet, library, and school ID cards with me at all times.
		32.	I arrive in class, take my seat, and get out my materials before the bell rings.
		33.	I have the following school supplies: pens, pencils, paper, binders, calculator, sticky notes, dictionary.
		34.	I ask others—friends, parents, teachers—to read, respond to, or check my work.
		35.	I ask the teacher for help when I do not understand an assignment.
		36.	I show my teacher and fellow classmates respect in the way I speak and act.
		37.	I greet my teachers when I enter the class and look them in the eye when I speak to them.
		38.	I have and seek adult allies and mentors who provide guidance and support when I need it.
		39.	I use different strategies to help me overcome difficulties I encounter in school and outside school.
		40.	I set and revise personal and academic goals for myself throughout the school year.
		41.	I contribute to class by asking questions, helping others, and participating in class discussions.
		42.	I set aside time for family and friends.
		43.	I complete and submit all assigned work on time.
		44.	I turn in original work (i.e., I do not plagiarize or cheat).
		45.	I am able to work on assignments and projects independently.
		46.	I make regular efforts to improve my academic and personal vocabulary.
		47.	I read—books, magazines, or newspapers—on my own outside of school.
		48.	I read the teacher's comments to improve my performance and understand my grade.
		49.	I study for quizzes and tests.
		50.	I take notes when teachers lecture, even if they don't require it.
			Total Score

FIGURE 1.3. Continued

May be copied for classroom use. School Smarts by Jim Burke (Heinemann, Portsmouth, NH); © 2004.

Success in school is not success in life, however. Throughout this chapter you have read of the habits of mind various people think lead to success in school and life. Making how we work and how we learn a valid, even essential, part of the curriculum is important so long as it is done in a way that yields results; so must the process by which people try to succeed. Success—teachers', students', athletes', leaders'—is not a mystery. Philosopher Tom Morris studied it. He opened his book *True Success* (1994) with a passage from Seneca that reiterates the role that "guides" (e.g., coaches, teachers, mentors, models) play in our success. Seneca, some two thousand years ago, wrote:

> First, therefore, we must seek what it is that we are aiming at; then we must look about for the road by which we can reach it most quickly, and on the journey itself, if only we are on the right path, we shall discover how much of the distance we overcome each day, and how much nearer we are to the goal toward which we are urged by a natural desire. But so long as we wander aimlessly, having no guide, and following only the noise and discordant cries of those who call us in different directions, life will be consumed in making mistakes—life that is brief even if we should strive day and night for sound wisdom. Let us, therefore, decide both upon the goal and upon the way, and not fail to find some experienced guide who has explored the region towards which we are advancing; for the conditions of this journey are different from those of most travel. On most journeys some well-recognized road and inquiries made of the inhabitants of the region prevent you from going astray; but on this one all the best beaten and the most frequented paths are the most deceptive. Nothing, therefore, needs to be more emphasized than the warning that we should not like sheep, follow the lead of the throng in front of us, traveling, thus, the way that all go and not the way that we ought to go. (14)

After studying the notion of success and the means by which people felt it was obtained throughout the centuries, Morris identified "the Seven Cs of Success":

1. A clear **conception** of what you want, a vivid vision, a goal clearly imagined. You can *see* what it is; you can *see* yourself accomplishing it.
2. A strong **confidence** that you can attain that goal.
3. A focused **concentration** on what it takes to reach your goal.
4. A stubborn **consistency** in pursuing your vision.
5. An emotional **commitment** to the importance of what you're doing.
6. A good **character** to guide you and keep you on a proper course.
7. A **capacity to enjoy** the process along the way.

The Four Cs of Academic Success

I admire and relish the clarity of Morris' model. It gives me such insight into people and achievements I've always respected. It gives me a framework even for my own efforts in the classroom and at home. Yet it doesn't have the simplicity I need to explain success to students; moreover, it lacks the kind of handle I need when designing instructional objectives or teaching my classes. Ultimately there is no one model, no One Way; each of us needs to find our own, to put this process and these ideas into our own language. Basketball coach John Wooden, for example, evolved over his career a now-famous Pyramid of Success that he taught to his players, something that helped account for their success on the court as much as in life after they left college (Wooden's pyramid may be viewed at *www.coachwooden.com*).

Explaining aspects of the pyramid, Wooden (1988) wrote:

> Now at the heart of the pyramid is *condition*. I stressed this point with my players. I don't mean physical condition only. You cannot attain and maintain physical condition unless you are morally and mentally conditioned. . . . I always told my players that our team condition depended on two factors—how hard they worked on the floor during practice and how well they behaved between practices. . . . At the very center—the heart of the structure—is *skill*. Skill, as it pertains to basketball, is the knowledge and ability quickly and properly to execute the fundamentals. Being able to do them is not enough. They must be done quickly. And being able to do them quickly isn't enough either. They must be done quickly and precisely at the right time. You must learn to react properly, almost instinctively. (90)

What does basketball have to do with academic success? Think about the kids who struggle and those who excel in your classes and school in general. They have not only skills but a level of fluency and automaticity that allows them to work efficiently, something academic classes and state exams demand. We know kids who have the skills but lack the stamina or the kind of commitment Wooden demanded and witnessed in his players.

Wooden's and Morris' ideas, along with those of many others, helped me recognize the pattern of success, the traits common to students who were succeeding in school. Borrowing from Morris' idea of Cs, I identified the Four Cs of Academic Success (see Figure 1.4).

Each of the following end-of-the-year letters illustrates various aspects of the Four Cs just outlined. All of these students were freshmen in my classes. Two of them were in my honors English class; the other two were enrolled in

THE FOUR Cs OF ACADEMIC SUCCESS

Commitment

Commitment describes the extent to which students care about the work and maintain consistency in their attempt to succeed.

Content

Content refers to information or processes students must know to complete a task or succeed on an assignment in class. Domains include academic, social, procedural, cultural, vocational, ethical, and cognitive.

Key aspects of **commitment** are:

- *Consistency:* Everyone can be great or make heroic efforts for a day or even a week; real, sustainable success in a class or on large assignments requires consistent hard work and quality conscience.
- *Effort:* Some students resist making a serious effort when they do not believe they can succeed. Without such effort, neither success nor improvement is possible.
- *Emotional investment:* Refers to how much students care about their success and the quality of their work on this assignment or performance. Directly related to perceived relevance and importance. This is what Jaime Escalante calls *ganas*, which means "the urge to succeed, to achieve, to grow."
- *Faith:* Students must believe that the effort they make will eventually lead to the result or success they seek. Faith applies to a method or means by which they hope to achieve success.
- *Permission:* Students must give themselves permission to learn and work hard and others permission to teach and support them if they are to improve and succeed.

Content knowledge includes:

- *Conventions* related to documents, procedures, genres, or experiences.
- *Cultural reference points* not specifically related to the subject but necessary to understand the material, such as:
  - People
  - Events
  - Trends
  - Ideas
  - Dates
- *Discipline- or subject-specific matter* such as names, concepts, and terms.
- *Features, cues, or other signals* that convey meaning during a process or within a text.
- *Language* needed to complete or understand the task.
- *Procedures* used during the course of the task or assignment.

FIGURE 1.4.   The Four Cs of Academic Success

May be copied for classroom use. School Smarts by Jim Burke (Heinemann, Portsmouth, NH); © 2004.

THE FOUR Cs OF ACADEMIC SUCCESS

Competencies

Competencies are those skills students need to be able to complete the assignment or succeed at some task.

Capacity

Capacities account for the quantifiable aspects of performance; students can have great skills but lack the capacity to fully employ those skills.

Representative, general **competencies** include the ability to:

- *Communicate* ideas and information to complete and convey results of the work.
- *Evaluate* and *make decisions* based on information needed to complete the assignment or succeed at the task.
- *Generate* ideas, solutions, and interpretations that will lead to the successful completion of the task.
- *Learn* while completing the assignment so students can improve their performance on similar assignments in the future.
- *Manage* resources (time, people, and materials) needed to complete the task; refers also to the ability to govern oneself.
- *Teach* others how to complete certain tasks and understand key concepts.
- *Use* a range of tools and strategies to solve the problems they encounter.

Primary **capacities** related to academic performance include:

- *Confidence* in their ideas, methods, skills, and overall abilities related to this task.
- *Dexterity*, which allows students, when needed, to do more than one task at the same time (aka multitasking).
- *Fluency* needed to handle problems or interpret ideas that vary from students' past experience or learning.
- *Joy* one finds in doing the work well and in a way that satisfies that individual's needs.
- *Memory*, so students can draw on useful background information or store information needed for subsequent tasks included in the assignment.
- *Resiliency* needed to persevere despite initial or periodic obstacles to success on the assignment or performance.
- *Speed* with which students can perform one or more tasks needed to complete the assignment or performance.
- *Stamina* required to maintain the requisite level of performance; includes physical and mental stamina.

FIGURE 1.4. Continued

my ACCESS class. All were successful, all ended the year having met not only academic but personal and social goals, which gave them each a sense of success that seemed a birthright to two and an elusive dream to the other two when they arrived in September. I asked them to write letters of advice to incoming freshmen to help them attain that same success.

Casey wrote:

Dear Freshman,

You are in for a very challenging and long year; although the advice I am going to give you in this letter will help you succeed in the days to come. In your 8th grade English class you probably breezed through the work with ease. Do not think you are going to breeze through this year's work. Do not come in this class thinking you are going to get an easy A, but come to this class ready to listen, think, and work. If you do those things you will end up with an A. After the first couple of months you will get used to the system and things will get a little easier for you.

To become a better student in the class you need to listen in class. I know it is hard to do, but if you have a friend in the class, try not to sit next to him/her. You will not be able to concentrate or listen to the teacher. If you are paying attention then everything will come easier to you. To get a better grade in the class just always do your homework because I know so many people who are getting Cs and Ds just because they do not do their homework. Probably one of the biggest setbacks of high school is drugs and alcohol. DO NOT get into that. There is no point and that stuff can really ruin your mind and mess up everything that was good about you.

Social life is a big thing to a high school student although many do not realize school is just as important. I believe that friends are everything and they get you through hard times, although school is the thing that will get you places. If there was a party on a Saturday night although you have not even started a project that was due on Monday, stay home and do the project. It will be tough to say no to the party although the feeling of finishing the project and having not to worry anymore is a great feeling. You can always be there for your friends although remember you always have to be there for your schoolwork.

The first year of high school is very fun and exciting but make sure you live it to the fullest because before you know it, the year is going to be over. If you think that things are too hard on you, just remember your family and friends will always be there for you. Remember that school is the most important and valuable thing you have so do not do things you think you will regret. Have a good freshman year and I guarantee if you follow my advice, your year will be one to remember.

Sincerely,
Casey Sturman

Mia Walker wrote:

Dear Freshmen Class of 2007,

On the first day of school, about a thousand papers will land on your desk in each class—material lists, rubrics, expectations, grading systems, rules, you name it. Beads of sweat will roll down your cheek, the air suddenly seeming heavier and hotter. Overwhelmed, you will then go to your counselor to be removed from honors classes because you realize this is too much for you. Your counselor will then tell you to give it two weeks, and if your mind does not change, then an adjustment can be negotiated. Trust me, your mind will change and honors will become your new home. Forget the papers stacked up on your desk, forget the essay on summer reading due in a week, forget the twenty-minute mile you just ran due to not running over the summer. It will get better and, by the end of the year, you will wonder how you ever survived without high school.

The keys to a successful year are organization and motivation. So many people told me that freshman year does not count for colleges or records, but they are completely wrong. Freshman year most certainly counts and brands you for the next four years. Shoot for a 4.0 GPA by completing all homework assignments, keeping your papers in order, remaining in control of all commitments, and remembering that high school is not all about social life. Have fun, but be a good student with clean and organized binders, and with a strong mental focus on what you are really here for—a good education.

Never take the easy way out. Do not skim books or articles; rather take helpful notes and do one hundred percent of every assignment. This way, tests will be much less stressful because you would have listened in class and processed information correctly. When taking tests, an answer will cross your mind instinctively and, usually, it is right. We all have semi-photographic memories, so by reading and concentrating thoroughly the answers will all store in your head. Study a sufficient amount, still, because information can be forgotten. Focusing and absorbing everything thrown at you in classes, however, will extremely help. By doing nothing less than one hundred percent in everything, the work will have gradually been done for you. You can never unlearn what you have learned, but you must learn it to begin with. The days when I did not completely pay attention in class turned out to be major losses, because I took steps backward in my progress and missed a lot of potentially important ideas. There exists nothing more frustrating than going home with complicated material explained in class, yet you failed to listen.

At the end of the year, I felt like a completely different person than the one who walked nervously into school the first day. I am more confident and less afraid of essays and projects. Everything became easy after I did it once. Just keep focused, surround yourself with awesome, supportive friends, and always do the hard tasks first. Then, the no-brainers will act as rewards and life will be less stressful.

Leave the inner eighth-grader inside you behind. You are in high school now and you must be more accepting and mutable. Freshman year is not the time to mess up, but to reinvent, discover, and learn from embarrassment. Trust me, soon, wearing an out-of-style shirt will not seem like such a big deal.

Sincerely,
Mia Walker

Ben Pierce wrote:

My experience here at Burlingame has been one hard trip. I had come to this school with a 5th grade reading level and now, now I'm close to being at a 9th grade reading level. My grades at the beginning of the year was a 1.0 GPA. Now, well I have a 2.67. And none of my grades from the second semester would have been so much better than my first semester if it wasn't for Mr. Burke. Mr. Burke not only taught me how to be a good student, but also taught me what it means to be a person. How to be a good person. If it weren't for my reading every morning and the worksheets that we've done, I wouldn't be as good as a test taker as I am now. I'm still learning of course, we as people will never stop learning, but Mr. Burke not only helped my intelligence but gave me a new mind to think with. I am not the same person I was a year ago. And if I was able to go back and change the mistakes in the past, I wouldn't change them. If not for my failures and bad decisions during the year, I would not be the person I am today. And I like that person. I thank myself of course but Mr. Burke too for showing me the way to success. He showed me the way by opening up my mind, making me realize that without an education, you've got nothing. And not just reading did he help me with, there's Algebra as well. When I was struggling in math, or didn't know how to do something, I'd just walk across the hall, and I would be helped. If I were to take a test, say for World History, there was Mr. Burke, my teacher, to help me, to show me how and what to study, even tell us why to study. And now at the end of the school year, I don't have to feel pressured about my report card.

Finally, Luba Kalinina wrote a speech titled "Believe in Yourself":

It took me fourteen years to learn one of the biggest lessons of my life. Do you really think things are possible if you don't think they are? If you have a goal in your life, you have to believe in yourself and not listen to others. Some people sit there and list what they can't do. It's not that they can't do it, they don't want to. You have to have a positive attitude about what you do because it's your life you're trying to improve.

Throughout my whole life I would try to learn new things like how to ride a bike or swim. I knew in my head that it's possible and that I could do it if I tried harder. If I just gave up and said I can't do it, maybe until this day I wouldn't know how to do the basic things in life. I see people every day complaining how they can't do things, and in my head I just think that they are lazy and are not even willing to try. Who says you have to be perfect and be able to do everything on the first try. It takes time and effort to reach a stage in your life where you can say you learned something because you believed in yourself.

Before learning this lesson I was one of those people who thought I couldn't do things just because I can't. Then I realized that all I do is give up, and you will not get anywhere in life if you keep giving up. Other people will be ahead of you because they believed in themselves from the beginning. Sometimes when I have a problem doing something I just tell myself that I can do it. I want to succeed in life and I know no one is going to sit here and do it for me. I have to build up my own steps to reach that point. This year I got one step closer because I knew I could bring my grades up if I wanted to and I did. I feel very proud of myself, but feel bad for people who are stuck at the stage where I was.

As long as you believe in yourself, no matter what other people think or say, you can do anything. I don't want to be the person that I was because I want to succeed in what I do. With the encouragement of people who are very close to me and mainly myself I know I can be what I want to be.

As if to validate all that she said, the local newspaper included a photo of Luba at our end-of-the-year celebration at the neighborhood elementary school where she and others in my ACCESS program had been going all year to work with the kindergartners, who, thanks to kids like Luba, will no doubt feel more at home in the country called School than Luba or Ben did when they first arrived in September. (See Figure 1.5.)

JUNE 3, 2003   THE INDEPENDENT   SERVING BURLINGAME AND HILLSBOROUGH

HOMETOWN

Teaming up for success

BHS Reading Buddies program may soon face elimination

BY SABRINA CRAWFORD
Independent Newspapers

BURLINGAME — Walking through the hallways of Washington Elementary, you can hear the laughter of children echo.

And once you step inside kindergarten teacher Alexia Bogdis' class, it's easy to see why.

Inside the alphabet-covered walls, children eagerly line up for fruit cups and juice — indicating that today something extra special is happening.

READING: page 11A

SUSAN CALDWELL
Burlingame High School teacher Jim Burke and BHS student Luba Kalinina listen to Washington Elementary kindergarten student Caroline Sharpe talk about how her mom had braided her hair, at an end of the year Reading Buddies party in the classroom of Alexia Bogdis.

FIGURE 1.5.   © Burlingame *Independent*. Reprinted with permission.

READING: BHS program may soon be eliminated

Continued from 3A

When a group of teens walk in, the kindergarteners wave their arms brightly,

"Hi, Ben. Hi. Monica. Sit next to me, Greg," they call out.

As the teen tutors scoot into kiddie chairs, books in hand, banging their adolescent knees against the too-tiny table tops, the 5-and-6-year-olds squeeze next to them and beam.

For Sue Glick, head of the Reading Buddies program, watching this kind of interaction is what makes her job so worthwhile. For the past seven years, Glick has built this program — which sends Burlingame High School teens to local elementary schools to help the young students learn to read and write. She's lovingly crafted it from the ground up.

But now, as the San Mateo Union High School District scrambles to find extra dollars amid the statewide budget crunch, Reading Buddies — and the entire community service learning program it's a part of — is on the chopping block.

PAWS (People, Action, Work, Service) was started in 1996 with special grant funding to help BHS students learn to serve in the wider community. Since then, Glick, also a BHS parent, has helped students organize food drives, fund-raisers, tutoring sessions and even a senior oral history project. But among the crown jewels has always been Reading Buddies.

"It's an amazing program." Glick said. "It takes a lot of coordination with the teachers to get them over here, but the kids and the teens both get so much out of it," she said.

But the original three-year grant has long since run out. In order to keep the $25,000 program going, the principal and parents agreed to fund it for one year. After that, the district took it over. But with SMUHSD looking to cut $4.5 million from next year's budget, special grant-launched programs like PAWS are facing the axe.

Now Glick fears her job and PAWS will come to an end unless BHS is able to find some alternate source of funding, such as a grant or private donor, to save the day. In the past few months, she's sent out several grant applications, appealed to local clubs and recently also to the BHS parent group who saved the program once before. Now, she's keeping her fingers crossed — that somebody will come through again.

"If we lose this, it's really going to have an impact," Glick said. "Not all kids learn by black-board teaching — some of them really need something else to help them along."

Bogdis, who has been teaching kindergarten for five years and participating in the Reading Buddies exchange for two, agreed. "I would hate to lose it next year," she said. "It really helps the kids. This way they get extra one-on-one attention that they can't get during regular class time."

On the other end of the spectrum, BHS English teacher Jim Burke said Reading Buddies enriches the lives of his students.

One of the first teachers to sign up for the program, Burke sends a small group of teens who have volunteered their study hall period twice a week to help Washington Elementary children learn to read.

"I've seen students grow so much in this program," Burke said. "Some of them have never been around young children. They may not have siblings and getting to mentor these kids — to have the chance to be tutors and role models — is so good for them."

One year, a junior he taught was so inspired that he and his classmates wrote a grant proposal — and raised $2,500 to buy books for their buddies.

Looking around the room, it's easy to see that this kind of spirit will carry on as long as the program continues.

At one table, kindergartener Brennan Lynch carefully fills in his journal. Wearing a navy 02 jersey, he bites down on his pencil and squints — trying to think of the right phrase.

"How do you spell 'because?," he asks 15-year-old freshman Ben Pierce.

Pierce looks back at him and smiles, "You know how, Brennan."

The younger boy looks a little uncertain but then sounds it out. "b-e-c."

"Keep going," Pierce encourages him.

"a-ummmm-u."

"That's right."

"s....e!" Brennan clamors triumphantly.

"All right," Pierce claps his hands. "See, you knew it."

Emboldened by his accomplishment, Brennan continues writing, then looks back up for a minute. "I did it, " he says. "I knew it!"

Pierce, who had never worked with children before Reading Buddies, is among those who think they may have found a true calling. "I really love working with little kids," he said. "They learn a lot from me helping them and I learn from them, too. I hope they don't end this, I really hope they don't."

FIGURE 1.5.   Continued

TWO
The Four Cs of Academic Success

Although some students show up at school as "intentional learners"—people who are already interested in doing whatever they need to do to learn academic subjects—they are the exception rather than the rule. Even if they are disposed to study, they probably need to learn how. But more fundamental than knowing how is developing a sense of oneself as a learner that makes it socially acceptable to engage in academic work.

—Magdalene Lampert, *Teaching Problems and the Problems of Teaching*

Personal Perspective

Sometimes we can best understand what we don't yet grasp by examining what we do. Studying failure is self-defeating in many cases; we want to know what *works*, not what doesn't. Researchers (Intrator 2003; Perry, Steele, and Hillard 2003; Marzano, Pickering, and Pollack 2001; Hrabowski, Maton, and Greif 1998; Langer 2002) focus more on who succeeds now and why, realizing, as Hrabowski et al. say, that much of the previous literature has focused on "deficiencies and weaknesses . . . instead of strengths. We believe that much can be gained by focusing on what produces success" (xii).

To understand my own academic experience and the Four Cs that follow, it seems most appropriate to study my most obvious and sustained success as a teenager: tennis. The Four Cs explain why I won, kept improving—and eventually traded my rackets for cameras, books, and, ultimately, the pen. The Cs also shed some light on why I was doing almost none of my schoolwork. The Four Cs do not, however, account for my passing grade in government, where someone—I swear it was not me!—stole Mr. Kernick's gradebook and he had to ask each of us what our grade was. I thought hard and suggested mine was about a D which he dutifully recorded and gave me on my report card.

How to explain my success in tennis in a way that accounts for my failure in school? The Four Cs offer some clues. Commitment, the first C, is essential; without it, the others don't matter. I committed myself to mastering tennis because I showed some talent, which allowed me to enjoy immediate satisfaction and subsequent rewards as a result of my efforts. Economists call such commitment economic behaviorism and use the term to explain people's decisions; in other words, they find that we make decisions based on what rewards us, what pays off. So long as it pays off, we keep making the same decisions. We therefore commit ourselves to the extent that we believe we will succeed, that the investment will make a difference. Bill Bradley (1998) calls this the "virtuous circle": "The harder you work, the sooner your skills improve. Then the virtuous circle takes over. As your skills grow, you get a rush of self-confidence, which spurs you to continue working, and your skills increase all the faster" (11). Writing on how the same virtuous circle applies to parents, Hrabowski et al. conclude: "What we do know is that the more attention we, as parents, give our [children], the higher our expectations of them, the more consistency in our approach to parenting, the greater our determination to work steadily with them, the greater the variety of educational and cultural experience we provide, the more likely they are to succeed" (1998, xi).

Not everyone accepts the premise that effort matters. Lauren Resnick (1999) observes, "Americans mostly assume that aptitude largely determines what people can learn in school, although they allow that hard work can compensate for lower doses of innate intelligence" (3). Resnick continues: ". . . what people believe about the nature of talent and intelligence—about what accounts for success and failure—is closely related to the amount and kind of effort they put forth in situations of learning or problem solving. [While some believe that intelligence is fixed, predetermined, and thus unchangeable,] others view ability as a repertoire of skills that is continuously expandable through one's efforts. Intelligence is incremental. People *get smart*. When people think this way, they tend to invest energy to learn something new or to increase their understanding and mastery" (4). This effectively sums up my experience in school and in life, beginning with tennis in high school.

My investment of time and energy—or, to use Tom Morris' term, my emotional commitment—led to success, which inspired me to persist so long as the efforts brought about success. This meant I was willing to do things—lift weights, run, jump rope—that I would not otherwise do in a million years; I did them because they delivered the success I sought. Hitting five hundred top-spin backhands down the line until I could repeatedly knock over tennis ball cans proved effective, as measured by my performance in matches and tournaments. Running a couple of miles every day gave me the stamina and strength others lacked, which meant more wins and, ultimately, deeper commitment.

By the time I arrived at high school, I was ranked among the top tennis players in California and experienced myself as a very successful, competent person. School seemed to offer only humiliation and failure, or at least struggle, and a feeling of disorientation. So I ignored it and committed myself to the domain (tennis) in which I excelled, thus reinforcing my identity as a successful person. In those few classes—Spanish, photography, woodshop—where I distinguished myself, I showed obvious commitment; I challenged myself and felt satisfied when I met those challenges. But it never occurred to me that the same commitment I made to tennis would translate into academic success if I applied the same principles of discipline, humility, and faith in my own ability to learn what was difficult and at times seemed impossible.

Out of this athletic commitment grew the other Cs: content, competencies, and capacity. I developed my content knowledge by reading everything I could get my hands on—repeatedly!—about tennis, the masters of the game, even the tournaments, such as Wimbledon. It all fed my commitment, like so much coal into the engine. If a match was on television, I didn't just watch it; I studied it. I read all the magazines. I gleaned content (i.e., knowledge about the game and how to play it) from anyone, anywhere; it all linked itself to the commitment and identity I was developing as a successful tennis player. I acquired and improved my competencies through daily, focused practice under the guidance of my coaches—Dave Harris, then Deepal Wannaqawatte, then Don Lowe, and finally, the inimitable Ralph Freund—to whom I gave complete permission to shape me into the athlete I wanted so badly to be. I developed my competencies through systematic practice against a range of carefully chosen opponents and through a series of regimens that resulted in the honing of specific shots that I could execute at will in competitive matches around the state. Capacity, as I mentioned already, resulted from my disciplined workout routine: running, lifting, jumping rope. Such rituals, along with frequent competition against better players, developed both my mental and my physical stamina, speed, and fluency. Out there under the 110-degree Sacramento sun, on courts 10 degrees hotter, I persevered, working with passion toward mastery of a game that eventually lost its magic as my commitment began to wane in the face of an obvious reality: I was good but would never be great. My identity of myself as a great tennis player gave way to mounting evidence that I was, within the world of my peers, average—capable of scaring, but never beating, the very top players.

Commitment is, in its rawest form, energy. Looking back on those years now, I see a seventeen-year-old boy who ignored school but began to wonder who and what he was if he wasn't a tennis player. Photography arrived at just that moment, a random course selection perhaps inspired by my father's love of photography, which provided an outlet for all that energy. If I couldn't get the school's prettiest girls to go out with me, I could at least get them to pose for me. An early award in a local contest for one of those photographs gave me the same sense of pride that knocking down those tennis ball cans had and ripping a winning cross-court backhand used to. Meanwhile, I was bombing Mr. Thorne's econ class, failing Ken Kitchener's English class, and making Mrs. Leach, my biology teacher, laugh just enough to ensure she would pass me.

On the rare occasions when I did study hard, I lacked any sense of commitment, due, as I remember it, to the feeling that it wouldn't make any difference. I enrolled in an SAT-prep class, but only because my two best friends and some cute girls did; instead of learning word roots and analogies, I spent the time cracking jokes and distracting the group, whose members, my friends included, came from college-educated parents that had instilled in them from early on the importance of school and education, and thus a commitment to a future they knew college would be sure to provide. I had little sense of commitment to either the class or the test, as the experience lacked any context for me; I didn't understand what it led to, so I celebrated my lack of content and competencies in ways that tested my friends' capacity for patience and friendship. They were committed, as were the others, because they understood that this test had nothing to do with analogies and everything to do with choices, with the life college would help them create for themselves. I had yet to learn that my life was, in fact, something I could create.

Months later, I watched those same friends drive away to the colleges that had accepted them, while I began the slow process of awakening, developing in myself the sense of purpose, the budding commitment to something I could not yet name. Later, when I stepped on to the campus at American River Junior College in Sacramento, I did so with a commitment to the only thing I understood at that point: the desire for a good life, a better life than the men and women I worked with at the printing shop had, a life made through choices that spawned in me—or would—a sense of deeper commitment and eventually an identity as someone who could "do school," could learn, could become what I had never been: a successful student.

THREE
Commitment

Y̦ou can be as good as you want to be, better

than you are, all you need is the desire and will to do it.

—Vince Lombardi

COMMITMENT describes the extent to which students care about the work and maintain consistency in their attempt to succeed.

Key aspects of academic **commitment** are:

Consistency: Everyone can be great or make heroic efforts for a day or even a week; real, sustainable success in a class or on large assignments requires consistent hard work and quality conscience. Some refer to this as craftsmanship, by which they mean the habit of excellence in both effort and quality of work.

Effort: Some students resist making a serious effort when they do not believe they can succeed. Without such effort, neither success nor improvement is possible. We will not try if we cannot possibly succeed; nor will we persist if we see no results from our efforts.

Emotional investment: Refers to how much students care about their success and the quality of their work on this assignment or performance. Directly related to perceived relevance and importance. This is what Jaime Escalante calls *ganas*, which means "the urge to succeed, to achieve, to grow."

Faith: Students must believe that the effort they make will eventually lead to the result or success they seek. *Faith* applies to a method or means by which they hope to achieve success.

Permission: Students must give themselves permission to learn and work hard and others permission to teach and support them if they are to improve and succeed.

Commitment: What It Is

All of the Four Cs apply equally to students, teachers, parents, and the educational institutions where students come to learn. How can we expect students to succeed if they are surrounded by people who do not expect and support such achievement? Summing up the importance of this first point, David Goslin (2003) argues that:

- Parents and their children must be persuaded to place a higher priority on academic achievement compared with other activities in their children's lives.
- Real academic achievement requires a great deal of hard work, much more than a majority of students are [currently] prepared to spend.
- [Parents, teachers, students, schools—and society at large] must modify beliefs about the relative importance of ability [versus] effort in learning, emphasizing the importance of hard work, as opposed to innate ability, for academic performance.
- Teachers as well as students must also come to believe that every student can learn even the most challenging subject matter and, indeed, is expected to succeed. (32)

Research on successful African American students (Hrabowski, Maton, and Greif 1998; Perry, Steele, and Hilliard 2003) echoes the previous list, citing "a strong commitment to education, an emphasis on self-help, the importance of a supportive learning environment in the home and in school, strong spiritual beliefs, supportive families, and a tradition of service to others" (Hrabowski et al. 1998, p. 14). Studying one successful African American student in an inner-city high school that suffers from an epidemic of failure (among other things), Ron Suskind (1998) illustrates the kind of commitment parents make to ensure their children's success:

> Barbara's . . . big decision was to quit her secretary's job and go on welfare. . . . She had been made a junior missionary at the church, and being with her Lavar in these crucial years was part of reordering her priorities. . . . She'd buy him books at the thrift shop . . . and cards with colors and numbers. . . . They'd sit while she flashed the cards and drilled him. They visited museums and the Anacostia library. Countless hours were spent in church. (31)

Of course, not all kids come to school with such supportive, committed parents. Consider this e-mail a teacher received from a committed foster mother whose foster son attended a successful suburban high school:

> Two weeks ago I dropped Esteban off at school and we haven't seen him since. Since then he has been with his "aunt" in Mt. View except on weekends. The trend for the last 3 or 4 weeks has been that he attends school during the week and then disappears on the weekends. I don't know if he simply doesn't want to return here or thinks he can't. My guess is the combination. I think you're correct is assuming this is a difficult time for Esteban. I can't imagine what it's like for a 14-year-old to have such bleak choices. His aunt lives with her partner in a one bedroom apartment. She already has Esteban's younger sister whose life makes Esteban's seem like a dream. While the aunt cares deeply for Esteban there just simply isn't room for him on a permanent basis and like our family, she does expect him to follow some basic rules. His mother was evicted from her apartment last week and according to the aunt they don't know how to contact her. Esteban can live with his father in San Francisco. It's not a perfect situation as his father has a "new" family and works a day and evening job. No wonder Esteban's angry and confused! As you know, he's not eligible to play football. I don't think he has anyone to talk to and I think any possible communication between you two can only be positive. I'm sure he thinks the rest of us are just telling him what to do. I just want Esteban to have the opportunity to lead a happy and healthy life.

Some students depend on their school to make the commitment to their success that parents have forgone. This tests the commitment of teachers in ways that are new and, for many, distressing, for many say they entered the profession to teach their subject, not to teach kids the skills needed to learn their subject. Mary Catherine Swanson, founder of AVID, came to a crossroads in her teaching career. After years of being one of the best teachers at an elite high school, Swanson accepted a position at a new school, where she committed herself to "prepare C students, who had little hope of going beyond high school, to take a college-prep curriculum" (Freedman 2000, 33). Swanson and her colleague Jim Grove reflected on their own work as teachers and concluded that "a teacher's role was to *meet* students' needs." They wondered, however, "how academically rigorous teachers *meet* poorly prepared students' [needs] . . . without sacrificing their own professional integrity and commitment to excellence? [They decided] they would have to improve students' learning skills, boost their self-confidence, and motivate them to take responsibility. They would require a mutual commitment between teachers and students" (32). This is the kind of commitment Robert Moses, civil rights leader and founder of the Algebra Project, describes in *Radical Equations* (Moses and Cable 2001) when he writes, "getting people at the bottom to make demands on themselves first, then on the system, that leads to the most important changes" (20). Another teacher, Jaime Escalante, expressed the commitment he exacted from his Advanced Placement calculus students at Garfield High School in an equation that he posted beside the clock: "Determination + Discipline + Hard Work = The Way to Success." Another poster over the blackboard extolled his watchword: *ganas*. The Spanish word loosely translates as "the urge—the urge to succeed, to achieve, to grow" (Mathews 1988, 191).

These teachers' examples raise an important angle on commitment that is worth exploring: internal versus external commitment. At some point, for commitment to become a way of life, a deeply held, guiding principle, we must internalize it, make it our own; it must become a part of our identity as teachers, parents, administrators—and, of course, students. Just as some students form identities of themselves as people who don't do school, or who can't succeed, others predicate their current and future identity on their success in school. They thus begin to externalize their commitment by what they *do* so that it accords with what they believe or feel; in this way, they develop first a private, then a public identity of themselves as a student, an academic performer. Schools as institutions, as well as teachers' and parents' expectations, contribute to these emerging academic identities, as Denise Clark Pope discovered in her book *"Doing School"* (2001). Her description of Faircrest High School shows us the standard for a community (the school is located near Stanford University) that collectively commits itself to students' success:

> [At Faircrest High] evidence of student success is everywhere. Teachers announce awards over the loudspeaker each morning: "Congratulations to Mr. Parker's class and the three winners of the state math competition . . . [names are read aloud]. Overall, Faircrest came in second, just behind Alpine School this year. Let's come in first next time!" The school sends dozens of letters home congratulating students who maintain 4.0 averages each semester. Teachers post the best essays and test results on classroom walls, hanging banners with names of students who earned perfect scores on advanced placement exams from the past ten years. And each month, every department honors an outstanding student, posting his or her photo on a central bulletin board and listing the names in the yearbook. In publications, on the walls, and over the loudspeakers, Faircrest's top students are impressive. They are articulate, focused, multitalented, and industrious. They are the pride of the public education system and the hope for the future. (3)

Compare Faircrest High with Ron Suskind's description of Frank W. Ballou Senior High, "the most troubled and violent school in the blighted southeast corner of Washington, D.C.":

> Their daily lesson: distinctiveness can be dangerous, so it's best to develop an aptitude for not being noticed. This, more than any other, is the catechism taught at Ballou and countless other high schools like it across the country. As with any dogma, however, there are bound to be heretics. At Ballou, their names are found on a bulletin board outside the principal's office. The list pinned up like the manifest from a plane crash, the names of the survivors. It's the honor roll, a mere 79 students—67 girls, 12 boys—out of 1,389 enrolled here who have managed a B average or better. . . . Giant, blocky blue letters now shout "WALL OF HONOR." The wall is a paltry play by administrators to boost the top students' self-esteem—a tired mantra here and at urban schools everywhere. The more practical effect is that the kids listed here become possible targets of violence, which is why some students slated for the Wall of Honor speed off to the principal's office to plead that their names not be listed, that they not be singled out. (1998, 33)

These two portraits of American high schools represent the kind of extremes Jonathan Kozol exposes in *Savage Inequalities* (1992) and Kathleen Cushman explores in *Fires in the Bathroom* (2003). What about a good "traditional school," in an average American suburb? Sam Intrator (2003) describes Stanton High School, which might rest somewhere between Faircrest and Ballou, as follows:

> Stanton's commitment to being a "traditional school" is apparent in the physical arrangement of many of the classrooms. In almost every one, the desks are aligned in rows facing forward; teachers stand front and center, their voices dominating; students are nearly silent. The walls are painted in antiseptic colors, are devoid of student work, are barely decorated aside from an occasional promotional poster from a book company; the whole school has an impassive, worn patina to it. . . . [One] student wrote: "Stanton High School is a long, boring book, a long-lasting obnoxious smell, a rude-awakening gong, a hot flame, a sound wave, a priority, and an alarm clock. Stanton is busy and quiet, cement stairs and uneven ramps, broken windows and tagged up bathrooms and piles of students, stuffy classrooms of large windows, lettering in gold, backpacks, benches, and tree stumps, and narrow, crowded hallways, and overheads and chalkboards. Its' students are stoners, skaters, bookworms, and average teens." (11)

Commitment is the engine that drives all other academic activity. We demonstrate and express our commitment through our expectations for ourselves, others, and the institutions whose job is to ensure our individual and collective success. The role of high expectations runs like an unbreakable thread through recent and past studies of academic success. Brian Blanton's spirited letter gives us some insight into how students respond to such high expectations. Brian entered high school reading two years below grade level and having a past of academic problems. Brian wrote this letter at the beginning of his second year of high school, after spending a year in my ACCESS program:

> Dear Mr. Burke:
>
> I'm not going to lie to you and tell you some bullcrap story. I have learned a lot this week because I realized that hey, these last three years are the best and most important part of my life. I'm saying this because if I screw up once, my life goals will go to shits. I know that I'm going to take these last three years very seriously cause I want to be somebody. I found myself these two weeks working hard towards my goals. I have been doing the best I can and let me tell you, it's working. Your class has helped me a bunch and I'm thankful for it. It seems like reality hit me this year. I'm more involved in school, I have more friends, I'm doing great in school, and I'm reaching *all* my goals. The biggest wonder for me was, how will I do this year on my tests? *Great* I told myself and that's how I want to keep it.
>
> When I write letters to you, I feel like I can say everything that I have learned, don't like, and have to learn. It's a great gift for me. When I write about goals on paper, I want to go back and write that I have achieved them.
>
> Always,
> Brian Blanton, Jr.

Jennifer Reyes provides a glimpse into the larger process by which a student feels the kind of commitment Brian describes (see Figure 3.1). Jennifer is writing about her first semester as part of the ongoing discussion in ACCESS about improvement; the program's commitment to ongoing improvement stems from the idea that reflection about what we are doing, why we are doing it, and how we are doing it is essential.

The ultimate evidence of commitment is when one takes a significant but personally meaningful risk in order to achieve some greater end. Such risks require genuine faith in not only oneself but the value of the goal that person is trying to achieve. Suskind (1998) describes the what he calls the "crab/bucket syndrome," when "one crab tries to climb from the bucket [and] the others pull it back down" (17). Public demonstrations of commitment become powerful indicators of a person's commitment to and acceptance of responsibility for their emerging identity; they are bold acts through which the person creates oneself, often at some cost. Lisa Marconi, a freshman in my ACCESS program,

August	Progress R#1	Jan 15	Jan 24 Access
	.	frustrated	successful
· excited/scared	· 2/4 educated	· nervous	· hardworker
· nervous	· Nervous but		· easy becau
· proud	· confident		Im doing &
· confident			what I have
· easy			2 do.
· happy			

When I arrived in August, I felt very excited but at the same time nervous. I felt this way because I was excited to enter high school, but nervous because I didn't know the school and everyone who came here. For example, at orientation we had to get in groups with people that had the same letter in your last name. For me it was "R" but most of the kids who were with me I did not know.

As the semester went by, I began to feel very strong and courageous to have been able to have gone through the first couple of days in getting to know my teachers and making new friends. So far everything has turned out to be just fine. Fortunately I know I have passed all my classes because I always ask teachers how I've been doing in class. Even though I was passing, homework and projects were still very hard. But because of my hard work, I went through it all just like I wanted to.

Finally, I was getting the hang of it. High school has now become a really fun place to be, especially when you're with friends. Now that the semester's started to finish, I began to feel good about myself and I also felt frustrated at the same time. The main reason why I felt frustrated was because finals occurred. I was stuck with many problems. For example, not understanding parts of History or Algebra. When the time came to take the tests (finals), I was still very nervous until I found out my grade. I didn't do so bad after all. So I felt more confident about myself and strong to have been able to pass my finals.

FIGURE 3.1.

enjoyed a very successful year, due to her commitment to her goals and her willingness to take risks en route to achieving those goals. See Figure 3.2 for what Lisa had to say about risk.

Others demonstrate their commitment by admitting to themselves—and others—that they have needs they cannot meet, weaknesses they cannot address on their own. Thus, they must give themselves permission to admit to these struggles and to ask others, such as teachers, to help them improve in those

Access... Room 82.

(good outcome)
(bad outcome)   (an opprotunity)
                    (A chance)
(lucky)   RISK
                    (brave)
(entertaining)   (crazy)   (dumb)
(scary)

9th grade Risk list
· standing up for myself
· participating in class
· getting up into a stunt w/ out hurting myself
· talking back to my mom
· telling the boy I'm talking to how I felt, and that I wasn't happy
· studying more
· driving a stick
· getting back with my boyfriend
· making new friends
· making stupid decisions
· going to Lincoln
· being a cheerleader

At the end of 8th grade, for so long I wanted to try out for the cheerleading squad at BHS, and I finally got my chance to. I ended up making the squad and I had some people that thought it was really stupid, but I also had many supporters.

As my freshman year at BHS has gone by, I've had to perform in front of the entire school, doing dance routines, and praying I wouldn't mess up. That for me feels so good. But there's also a bad side to it. I get made fun of, people think we're annoying, when what we're doing is supporting our athletic teams. We spend hours and hours trying to get our routines perfect, and our jumps higher than before, and getting our stunts up without falling, it makes me so mad when people say that cheerleading isn't a sport because I might not work hard to run faster or throw a ball further. I spend so much time trying to learn dances and to kick and jump higher and get thrown in the air. I'd like to see a football player do that.

And that's what keeps me going.

FIGURE 3.2.

areas. Greg Chong, a boy who entered high school (and my ACCESS program) reading at the fifth-grade level, wrote the following letter after a year of hard work during which he committed himself to learning what he needed to know if he was to succeed in high school.

Dear Mr. Burke,

There has been a great progress in my reading capability and speed. An example of that is in my reading speed. I have gone from eight pages in fifteen minutes to an average of twenty pages in fifteen minutes. Also, my study habits have gotten to a higher level of learning. Now I am studying smart and not just longer for my history tests, which I always knew I couldn't remember all of it and start forgetting the important stuff to put in all of the pointless stuff. I went from getting a D and F on my tests to getting an A, B or C on the tests. These high test scores have led me to a current B+ in the class shooting for an A on the final. Nothing has really changed in math because I am in such a low math class that it all just came too easy for me that it resulted in an A at the end of the first semester.

Now that I can look back and see what I was doing wrong and how to fix it, I now know what success really is and how to achieve it to get my goal. I can now see how much this class not only helped me as a student, but also has helped me build my own character. Now I know that just a little practice of doing something right is better than doing a lot of something wrong and to want to get something right the first time.

Now as a student, I feel confident enough to go into a classroom and not be afraid to sit in the front row and ask questions about something I don't quite understand. Now I know I can learn anything I really want too if I put my mind into doing it. I will apply myself to do the things that will help me to succeed in school and in my future life to come.

At the end of this year, I will leave this class but I will not leave this class without learning an important life lesson. Thank you Mr. Burke for helping me pass my first year of high school. I will never forget your class and the lessons I learned in it.

Greg Chong

I end this section with an exchange between me and a sophomore. I think the letters—my letter to the class and Maria Perez's subsequent response to it—say it all:

Dear Fifth Period:

I find it helpful to stop what I am doing periodically and think about my classes in light of the questions you yourselves have answered recently: Where am I? Where do I want (us as a class/you as students/me as a teacher) to be?

How can I make that happen? Without these questions how can I ever be the teacher I dream of being, the parent I need to be, the husband I am supposed to be, the person I want to become?

When I called in the journals today, I was stunned to see only sixteen journals from a class of thirty-six students. Moreover, I was genuinely disappointed to see only seven of the journey poems turned in when I gathered them. While I said I will allow the poems to be turned in tomorrow, I will not accept late journals (unless you were legitimately absent). They were due last Friday; I have already given you an extra two days.

But I wonder why this happens. Most would argue laziness. Fine. Others might say they did not understand, so they did not do them. It is always okay not to understand; it is never acceptable to not do the work. Coming to me to say you need help is your obligation, it is part of your work. To give yourself permission not to do your work, or to do it poorly, is to betray yourself.

We have discussed two ideas in the last few days that seem to intimidate some people: standards and satisfaction (with your life as you now live it). I have established standards which might challenge you, but they are also standards you can meet, which you must meet. My job is to help you reach them; your performance in this class is the best measure of my own success. Thus when I see less than half the class turn in their work today, I cannot count myself successful.

Where we are: We have established a tradition of good discussions about significant ideas. We have had the chance to write about a wide range of ideas and topics that matter to the society at large and to you as individuals. We are beginning a challenging novel; as we read it you will have nightly reading, daily writing, and a large ongoing project. Depending on what grade you want to be eligible for, you are reading outside books which you will write one essay about before the semester is over.

Where we need to be: All work done as and when assigned. Everyone here every day. Having fun. Enjoying the work of our minds as we develop our ability to write, read, speak, and think. Taking ourselves seriously as students, teachers, people.

We tend to be our own obstacles to the success we seek. Letting you turn in work you will do sloppily at the last minute offers you no help. Only by doing tonight's homework, and tomorrow's, and the next day's will you change your standing and achieve the success you want.

It's hard work to be good—in a subject, at a job. It's time you grew up a bit, those of you who aren't doing your best. The world expects it of you; you need to expect it of yourself. In the meantime, I will be doing everything I can to be the best teacher I know how to each of you; and when I fail, when I fall, I will study my bruises and scrapes to see what they have to teach me. And I will be getting up every morning, glad that I get to work with you. Will you be able to choose what you do for a living when you're my age—or will you let your life happen to you? Get behind the wheel of your life and go somewhere.

Here's Maria's response:

Dear Mr. Burke,

I don't understand why you care. I think it's that person's decision if they want to get a bad grade. I am one of the persons that didn't turn in a poem. I didn't do it because I was too lazy to think poetically. I got scared of writing a poem. When I was a 5th grader, I would write poems because I was depressed and I felt that by writing a poem, it would bring back those bad feelings. It's no excuse, and I'm sorry.

I personally like your class and also enjoy the class discussions. I will try to live up to the standards in your class. Thank you for this wake-up call.

Sincerely,
Maria Perez

As a brief postscript to Maria's letter, I can't resist telling you how things turned out. She graduated and enrolled first in a community college, where she worked hard, taking general education classes to prepare for the state college, which accepted her. There, she studied business, intending to return to Nicaragua and open up a business that would benefit the community she and her family had fled years before. I found all this out when she was visiting my school to get transcripts to apply for graduate school. Each success along the way had emboldened her to reach a bit higher, and so the cycle of success ran its course, teaching her that anything was possible if she worked hard enough.

What Factors Affect Commitment?

Commitment is not a fixed point, not a state of mind we occupy full-time; rather, it is a continuum along which we move, depending on the task, its demands, and our own feelings about the work. Numerous factors directly impact our commitment, preventing us from moving farther along the continuum or hurling us to the farthest end of commitment. I will discuss them in greater detail, but a short and inevitably incomplete list of such factors includes:

- Identity
- Allies
- Engagement

Identity
Identity is best represented by a comment a student of mine once made while on a field trip to a local community college. I took a group of girls to a Latina

literature conference at the college. After getting out of my van, the girls stood looking around at the campus. No one in their families had ever gone to college. They did not expect to go, even though they were taking college-prep classes. Paulina, a freshman who was at that time making great progress and has since gone to college, said, "Oh my God, they look just like me!" It came as an involuntary gasp, barely whispered. I wondered what she thought people who go to college looked like. As a new high school student, Mike Rose (1989) took vocational education classes, going where he was told, not knowing to question his placement. Rose, whom the school mistakenly placed in the vocational program, wrote, "You're defined by your school as 'slow'; you're placed in a curriculum that isn't designed to liberate you but to occupy you, or, if you're lucky, train you, though the training is for work the society does not esteem" (28).

Identity is, indeed, a fundamental aspect of developing and maintaining commitment. We must be able to see ourselves doing what someone asks us to do; as I often tell my ACCESS students, "To be it, you must see it." Speaking once to a former ACCESS student who went on to be president of the school's La Cultura Latina organization after he addressed a library full of Latino parents, I told him how proud I was; his immediate response was one of wonder, saying, "I never saw myself doing any of this stuff!"

"Well now you can," I told him, "and it will lead you to other things, because you know you are someone who can lead, who can work hard, who can speak to people, who can get them involved."

This notion of identity extends to the very language we use to describe ourselves. "Oh, I'm just not a math person," we say; "I'm not a good test taker," students in my ACCESS program tell me, giving themselves permission to keep failing. Thus, my challenge is to help them see that they *can* do these things— write, give speeches, succeed on tests, read—that they formerly "couldn't do." In *Reading for Understanding* (Schoenbach et al. 1999), the authors report "that having a sense of who one is as a reader [is] an important aspect of motivation. Especially for students who think of themselves as nonreaders or poor readers, developing a sense of *reader identity* is crucial" (28). Lampert (2001) speaks of developing an "academic character" and an "academic disposition"; she continues, saying, "One's sense of oneself as a learner is not a wholly private construction. Academic identity is formed from an amalgamation of how we see ourselves and how others see us. . . . Because the relationships in a classroom occur among the same set of people, in a public setting, daily, and over a long period of time, they offer multiple occasions for self-expression and have a strong potential to influence self-perception. . . . If a student does not see himself or herself as the kind of person who is going to learn, it seems unlikely that learning will occur" (265).

As Lampert and the others make clear, commitment is essential to success; indeed, we will rarely even try something unless we feel we can do it (Costa and Garmston 2001). This reluctance plays a key role in determining students' commitment; researchers studying the "self-defeating behaviors" of failing students found that the more schools stress achievement (instead of learning and improvement), the more kids "go to great lengths to avoid looking 'stupid' in front of teachers or classmates—even if it means undermining themselves in the process" (Viadero 2003). Such findings have other implications: boys who go to schools where all the teachers are women and the kids who do best are girls might see school or such related activities as a "girl thing"; poor and working-class children who do not see themselves represented in challenging activities, clubs, or advanced classes will think they are not worthy or capable of such performances; and African American or Latino students who do not see examples of successful peers at home, in the community, in the media, or around school may well come to believe that school success is not for them, that they don't "do school." The extent to which we are willing to risk the humiliation that often accompanies real growth often depends on whether we have allies, people who can help us sustain our commitment.

Allies

Throughout his book *Lives on the Boundary* (1989), Mike Rose comments on the role mentors and advocates played in his own academic journey; these allies not only inspire in him a feeling of commitment but help him sustain and even grow that commitment over time. "To journey through the top levels of the American educational system will call for support and guidance at many, many points along the way," Rose asserts. "You'll need people to guide you into conversations that seem foreign and threatening. You'll need models, lots of them, to show you how to get at what you don't know. You'll need people to help you center yourself in your own developing ideas. You'll need people to watch out for you" (48). Many other authors and studies report something similar: successful students, like great athletes, find the academic equivalent of coaches, who coax and push, guide and advise as the student learns to feel at home in this new country. Such allies are especially essential for those who come from working-class backgrounds or families in which no one has attended college. In "This Fine Place So Far from Home," Laurel Johnson Black (1995) describes her teachers' efforts to help her and other students enter the larger world of academic study:

> My teachers tried to bridge the gap with speech. "In other words," they said, looking from the text to us, "What they're saying is . . ." They tried to bridge the gap between their bodies, one hand pointing to the board, the other hand stretched out palm up, fingers trying to tug words from mouths contorted with the effort to find the right speech. We were their college-bound students, the ones who might leave, might be them again, might even do better. They were like our parents in their desire to have us succeed, but they had skills and knowledge that counted to the white-shirted men who sat behind the glass windows at the savings and loan. . . . I wanted to be like my teachers. (18)

The importance of such mentoring is not new, of course. Seneca wrote about it almost two thousand years ago:

> So long as we wander aimlessly, having no guide, and following only the noise and discordant cries of those who call us in different directions, life will be consumed in making mistakes—life that is brief even if we should strive day and night for sound wisdom. Let us, therefore, decide both upon the goal and upon the way, and not fail to find some experienced guide who has explored the region towards which we are advancing; for the conditions of this journey are different from those of most travel. (Morris 1994, 15)

Some allies meet other needs students may not know how to meet on their own. Many students who are trying to form new patterns and achieve previously elusive levels of success need a sanctuary, a shelter where they find resources, materials, space, peace, acceptance, and support. Jaime Escalante provided this in his room, which became a kind of intellectual refuge for his kids. The science teacher in Suskind's *A Hope in the Unseen* (1998) provides a similar retreat for Cedric Jennings. Only in Mr. Taylor's chemistry classroom can Cedric find what he needs to maintain his commitment while at school: "It's [Cedric's] private sanctuary, the only place at Ballou [High School] where he feels completely safe, where he can get some peace. . . . Mr. Taylor has personally invested in Cedric's future since the student appeared in his tenth grade chemistry class" (7). Such rooms become more than classrooms; they take on the feeling of a community, a small island that accommodates those few who share certain values, dreams, or needs.

In *Making the Most of College: Students Speak Their Minds*, Light (2001) concluded that such relationships were one of the most important factors in students' success. When asking incoming freshman students, "What's your job?"

Light dismisses their immediate assertion that their job is "to work hard and do well," and tells them that their job is to establish a relationship with one adult by the year's end: "I share with them the single most important piece of advice I can possibly give to [freshmen]: 'Your job is to get to know one faculty member reasonably well this semester, and also to have that faculty member get to know you reasonably well'" (86). One way teachers demonstrate their own commitment to students is by providing such retreats, extending such hospitality to students so that school becomes a place where these students feel known, cared for, welcomed, encouraged, supported. Intrator (2003) writes about one high school teacher, Mr. Quinn, whom students describe thus: "What they like best about Mr. Quinn is his commitment to hard work for and with them. As one student said, 'He really tries to learn with us, not just teach us.' Another said, 'I sometimes get the feeling that Mr. Quinn learns from us. I know he's really smart and wise, but sometimes during class conversation, I just think he's learning from us. Whether he really is, or not, doesn't matter as much as it seems as if he is trying to learn from us'" (13).

Engagement

If students see themselves as capable, as people who engage in the type of activity the teacher assigns; if they know they have allies they can turn to, can count on to help them successfully complete the assigned task; if these needs are met, it is likely that students will not only do the work but actively engage both emotionally and intellectually, working with a sense of craftsmanship, a conscience about the quality of the work. The level of engagement that Csikszentmihalyi (1991) calls "flow" captures best the relevant aspects of engagement. Jeff Wilhelm (2003), summarizing the "conditions of [the] 'flow' experience," says that an engaging task or curriculum must have:

- A clear purpose, goals, and immediate feedback
- A challenge that requires an appropriate level of skill and assistance to meet the challenge (as needed to be successful)
- A sense of control and developing competence
- A focus on immediate experience
- The importance of the social

Asking himself, "What kind of curriculum meets these demands?" Wilhelm answers: "a learning centered curricular structure that assists students to ask their own questions, solve problems, and create knowledge artifacts that do 'social work.'" In their book *Reading Don't Fix No Chevys* (2002), Smith and Wilhelm specifically examine boys' engagement with school and, in particular, reading. "Several boys . . . reported that reading didn't give them that feeling [of competence and control]. Mark explained why he ranked reading so low: 'It feels like it is almost a waste of time because you're not accomplishing anything'" (33). Citing findings from the work of Elaine Millard (1997), Smith and Wilhelm add that "boys are disadvantaged in academic literacy as a result of current curricular emphases, teacher text and topic choices, and lack of availability of texts that match their interests and needs" (14).

In *Tuned in and Fired Up: How Teaching Can Inspire Real Learning in the Classroom*, Intrator (2003) examines one high school English teacher over the course of a full school year. The analysis includes students' critiques of assignments, activities, and the class in general. Intrator strives to answer the question of when students "tune in" and get "fired up." He sums up his observations of the class when he writes, "The students in Mr. Quinn's class were most alive, most engaged, most provoked when they were generating ideas, insights, and understandings of the world. These moments are what Joseph Campbell calls the 'rapture of being alive,' and they came about as a 'live encounter' between subjects and the students." Intrator concludes by saying, "In my research these moments of inspired learning shared certain elements: when a teacher stirred the interest of a student so that the student tuned in and discovered an emotional attachment to the subject. When this connection occurred, students got fired up in ways that allowed them to brim over with ideas that altered their view of themselves and the world" (132).

Remember: the Four Cs apply to teachers as much as students. Many teachers feel that engaged learning is not possible in a standards-based curriculum; others feel disengaged when the textbook or other prescribed curriculum strips them of their creative role in the classroom. In his book *An Ethic of Excellence: Building a Culture of Craftsmanship with Students* (2003), Ron Berger writes, "Much of the country seems seduced at the moment with visions of *teacher-proof* curriculum, where teachers are seen as little more than semi-skilled gas station attendants *delivering curriculum* into student brains" (11).

Indeed, many teachers feel that standards undermine their own sense of engagement. Attending my sons' Back to School Night recently, I couldn't help notice the way the teachers spoke about the inquiry-based projects and simulations they had previously done but could not do this year "because of the standards" and all they had to do to meet them. Ironically, it appears that many of the efforts to "close the achievement gap" and "improve student performance" are undermining teachers' *and* students' commitment to school—but not their passion for learning: many are simply learning what matters to them outside of school. Suarez-Orozco and Gardner (2003), discussing a hypothetical student named Billy, write: "When Billy's teachers began 'teaching to the test,' preparing for state assessments and College Board exams dominated the curriculum. Billy's cognitive engagement and excitement came wholly from extracurricular activities—from his love of computers and a growing passion for Chinese history. Billy—like millions of kids in American classrooms—got bored. The failure to harness Billy's contagious energy is the failure of an education system more in tune with the realities of early 20th century America than with the demands of the 21st global century. And the bad news is that the standards movement with its incessant mantra—test, test, test—is likely to transform the boredom bug into a national epidemic" (44). The authors offer their own recommendations for engendering flow, saying "that increasing the engagement of students in academic learning means reducing somewhat the amount of time and energy that our children devote to a wide range of competing demands, including athletics and the acquisition of other non-academic skills, watching television or using computers, engaging in social activities, dating, and employment after school. It also means placing more emphasis on the importance of hard work as opposed to innate ability, for academic performance; increasing the availability of rewards for such hard work; and working to incorporate best practices in our schools" (34).

Full engagement means deep commitment, sustained motivation; the activity must meet a range of human needs. Loehr and Schwartz (2003) offer a dynamic model of the "corporate athlete," which we might adapt for the current discussion to the "academic athlete": The challenge of great performance is to manage your energy more effectively in all dimensions to achieve your goals. Four key energy management principles drive this process. They lie at the heart of the change process . . . and are critical for building the capacity to live a productive, fully engaged life. Principle one: Full engagement requires drawing on four separate but related sources of energy: physical, emotional, mental, and spiritual. Human beings are complex energy systems, and full engagement is not simply one-dimensional" (9). Osborn and Osborn (1997) provide the following list of common human needs we must meet if we are to be happy and willing to engage:

Comfort	Having enough to eat and drink, keeping warm when it's cool and cool when it's warm, being free from pain.
Safety	Feeling secure in your surroundings, being protected from crime, surviving accidents and natural disasters, having an environment free of pollutants.

Control	Having a hand in your own destiny, planning for the future, fixing things and people, influencing or directing others, controlling your environment.
Tradition	Having a sense of roots, having a feeling of continuity with the past, doing things as they have always been done, honoring your forebears.
Friendship	Establishing warm relations with others, being a member of a group or organization, being accepted by others, having someone to love and be loved by.
Nurturance	Taking care of others, comforting those in distress, aiding the helpless, caring for animals, giving to charitable organizations, providing volunteer service.
Recognition	Being treated as valuable and important, having your achievements praised by others, receiving trophies or awards, being the center of attention.
Success	Accomplishing something of significance, overcoming obstacles to achieve your goals, doing better than expected, reaching the pinnacle of your profession.
Independence	Being able to stand on your own, being self-sufficient, making your own decisions, being your own person.
Variety	Longing for adventure, visiting new and unusual places, trying different things, changing jobs, moving to a new town, meeting new people.
Curiosity	Understanding the world around you, understanding yourself, understanding others, questioning why things happen or why people act as they do, finding out about the unusual.
Enjoyment	Doing something just for the fun of it, taking a vacation, pampering yourself, pursuing a hobby. (104)

Writing about the "quiet crisis in boys' literacy," Tom Newkirk (2003) noted that the difference between girls' and boys' performance on the 2003 twelfth-grade NAEP (National Assessment of Educational Progress) reading scores was the same as the gap between African American and white students in the twelfth grade. "By the 12th grade, male scores were on average 24 points lower than female scores—and almost three-fourths of this gap had been opened up by grade 4" (34). Newkirk ends his commentary by recounting his early years of teaching. Note how many of the human needs listed earlier—as well as those ideas Intrator discusses—apply to Newkirk's story:

> In my first year of teaching, [my students resisted the required reading] in an all-boys high school in Boston. I called my dad that first night in a panic. How could I make it through a year, when students refused to read the anthology (and a few used it as a projectile)? He asked me the simple question, "What will they read?" I explained to him that I didn't think there was anything in the musty book closet that they would voluntarily read.
> "I'm not talking about the book closet. What *will* they read?"
> After some hesitation, I said that they might read *Sports Illustrated*.
> "Well, tomorrow morning you buy every *Sports Illustrated* you can find and take them to class."
> I followed his advice, raiding all the newsstands in my neighborhood. The students did read. It was not a miraculous *Dead Poets Society* turnaround, but a good step in the right direction. (34)

In *Designing a New Taxonomy of Educational Objectives*, Marzano (2001) offers six levels of processing (see Figure 1.2). The one most relevant to engagement is the highest level: self-systems processing, which Marzano describes thus:

> This model not only describes how human beings decide whether to engage in a new task at some point in time, but it also explains how information is processed once a decision to engage has been made.
> In this theory, a "new task" is defined as an opportunity to change whatever one is doing or attending to at a particular time. For example, assume that Lisa is in a science class, daydreaming about an upcoming social activity after school. At that moment, her energy and attention are on the social activity. However, if her teacher asked her to pay attention to some new information that was being presented about science, she would be confronted with a decision regarding a new task.
> The self-system contains a network of interrelated beliefs and goals . . . and is also a prime determiner in the motivation one brings to a task. If a task is judged important, if the probability of success is high, and positive affect is generated or associated with the task, the individual will be motivated to engage in the new task. If the new task is evaluated as having low relevance and/or low probability of success and has an associated negative effect, motivation to engage in the task is low. To be motivated to attend to the new science information, then, Lisa would have to perceive the information as more important than the social event, believe she can comprehend the information, and have no strong negative emotions associated with it. . . .

Finally, relative to any new task, success is highly dependent on the amount of knowledge an individual has about that task. For example, the extent to which the science student achieves her learning goals would to a great extent depend on her prior knowledge about the science topic. (11)

Marzano's final words build a bridge to the second of the four Cs: content. If content were viewed as a mountain, commitment would refer to the desire one has to climb that mountain. As with all things, some see a mountain and its challenges as an interesting invitation, an opportunity to achieve something; others see it instead as an obstacle, a problem they don't want to—or "can't"—solve. As many have said in different ways, you can't fail if you don't try. Thus, to withhold commitment to learning content that is difficult is to stay, for the time being, safe and secure. Committing to greater success in schools, especially for those students whose friends are not committed to such success, therefore involves risks. Pedro Noguera (2003), writing about his son Joaquin's "dilemma" and that of other urban students of color he studied, reports: "In these schools, high-achieving students of color, like my son Joaquin, are sometimes unwilling to enroll in Advanced Placement courses or engage in activities that have traditionally been associated with White students because they fear becoming estranged from their friends. If they appear to engage in behavior that violates racial norms, they may be seen as rejecting membership in their racial group and run the risk of being regarded as race traitors" (23). This is the previously mentioned phenomenon that Ron Suskind (1998) calls "the crab/bucket syndrome: when one crab tries to climb from the bucket, the others pull it back down" (17).

Our challenge is to improve and expand the means by which kids can form meaningful, effective connections with teachers through not only personal relationships but content that speaks to the person they are and the one they are trying to become. This means not only connecting to students through content but teaching and developing in them the competencies they need to access, remember, and *use* that content to achieve those goals to which they have finally committed themselves.

FOUR
Content

Content is king.

—Bill Gates

I have a dream that my four little children will one day live

in a nation where they will not be judged by the color

of their skin, but by the content of their character.

—Martin Luther King, Jr.

CONTENT refers to information or processes students must know to complete a task or succeed on an assignment in class, or in school in general. Domains include academic, social, procedural, cultural, vocational, ethical, and cognitive.

Content knowledge includes:

Conventions related to documents, procedures, genres, or experiences.

Cultural reference points not specifically related to the subject but necessary to understand the material, such as:

- People
- Events
- Trends
- Ideas
- Dates

Discipline- or subject-specific matter such as names, concepts, and terms.

Features, cues, or other signals that convey meaning during a process or within a text.

Language needed to complete or understand the task.

Procedures used during the course of the task or assignment.

The honors and Advanced Placement English teachers gather in Diane McClain's summer sunlit room in late August days before school begins. We've come together to discuss the AP English teacher's concern that students come to her lacking the knowledge they need to read poetry and succeed on the AP test. Some protest, others defend, still others look out the window as if recalling the pleasant hours of the summer that is winding down by the minute. The kids need to know certain terms, ideas, and strategies when it comes to poetry; there just isn't time for Elaine, the AP teacher, to pack all that content into the months prior to the test, not with everything else she has to teach.

"I thought it would be a good idea to give you some sense of what the test is like, what the kids have to know if they are to succeed on the exam. So I ran off some copies of one sample portion, one with a poem by Elizabeth Bishop, and thought we could just take it and see how we do," says Elaine in a friendly manner. Now everyone *knows* summer is over; people begin stirring, a couple utter, "Ohh . . . ," or "Well, what a surprise . . . ," and the like. The air thickens a bit with tension; everyone wants to do well, of course. After all, it's a test! So we launch into reading Bishop's "One Art" and taking the three-page exam. When we discuss the test and the poem, what surfaces is that most of us simply lack content knowledge about poetry. The first question asked, Which of the following answers best describes the rhyming pattern of the poem? The correct answer, a villanelle, did not occur to most people because they simply did not know it.

This scene, which involves a circle of excellent, committed English teachers, illustrates the issue of content effectively. Part of the content is the teacher's knowledge of terms, of the literary tradition and the reading of poetry in a general sense. The AP teacher's investment in her content knowledge included an understanding of not only the forms but the poet and the places and people Bishop alludes to in the poem. The National Board for Professional Teaching Standards (NBPTS) recognizes the importance of such professional content knowledge in the second of the Adolescence and Young Adulthood/English Language Arts Standards (2003): "Accomplished Adolescence and Young Adulthood/English Language Arts teachers have a thorough command of the various domains of knowledge that compose the English language arts" (13). The NBPTS document continues, saying that accomplished teachers "have an impressive command of the various domains of knowledge that comprise the English language arts, and, as lifelong learners, they deepen their content knowledge through continual study and accumulated practical experience in the classroom. In this way, their command of the theory, research, and practice in the various domains of the field are all brought to bear for the benefit of student learning" (13). The NBPTS' second "core proposition" states that all "teachers know the subjects they teach and how to teach those subjects to students" (vi).

Content: What It Is

No one argues whether kids should learn or not; not so with content. Everyone has an opinion about *what* students should learn, and most have good reasons behind their claims. Mortimer Adler's Great Books program invites us all to join in the Great Conversation; who wouldn't want their child to be reading some of the most important books and discussing them with peers, led by trained teachers posing insightful questions? E. D. Hirsch's Core Knowledge (aka Cultural Literacy) theory asserts the centrality of certain texts, facts, and general knowledge as a means of being able to understand what we hear, read, and see in the newspapers and the books we read. Others—Maxine Greene, Eliot Eisner, Howard Gardner—lobby for the arts, contending that the study of "the true, beautiful, and the good" (Gardner 1999, 19) creates people who "understand the world, who gain sustenance from such understanding, and who want—ardently, perennially—to alter it for the better. Such citizens only come into existence if students learn to understand the world as it has been portrayed by those who have studied it most carefully and lived in it most thoughtfully" (20).

Coalition of Essential Schools programs call for deep investigations of "essential questions" related to central issues and subjects that are important to society. Some (Ravitch 2003; Hirsch 1988; Stotsky 1999; Sykes 1995) argue for content that targets skills and improves background knowledge instead of self-esteem or cultural awareness. Of course some (Greer and Kohl 1995) offer opposing recommendations, anchoring their suggestions in those texts and ideas that will prepare students to live in a diverse, global society. Still others (Reich 1992; Friedman 1992) take this notion of global education a step further, describing students as "knowledge workers" and "arbitrageurs" of information.

Those schools and communities that focus on admissions to the most prestigious universities look to such tests as the Advanced Placement exam, the SAT, and the ACT for guidance as to the proper content to teach; the SAT, in fact, now reflects the content taught in the high school classroom so as to improve alignment between secondary and higher education. But many universities around the country have begun to express their frustrations with the lack of content knowledge (and associated competencies) students bring to their college courses; thus, universities have begun publishing a string of high-profile reports that lay out what students should know if they are to succeed in college.

While these different scholars, programs, and reports offer useful and important guidelines for what students should learn, it is the textbook publishers that exert the most profound influence on what teachers teach and students learn, a fact that Diane Ravitch (2003) finds reprehensible, especially as these textbooks are, according to Ravitch, guided not by educational excellence but by cultural sensitivity. "The [textbook] guidelines, when faithfully applied, guarantee the exclusion of imaginative literature from our textbooks. They actively prohibit the transmission of our national culture, whose imaginative literature was not written in conformity with the publishers' language codes. They assume that everything that was not written in accordance with their mandates must be racist, sexist, ageist, and harmful to any group that has ever known oppression or exclusion. Is it any wonder that students who read such pap do not enjoy reading, and that they see little connection between art and life? The [textbook publishers'] guidelines discredit the educational mission of the school in the eyes of the young" (49).

What *is* the content that students need to succeed in the classroom and the workplace when they eventually enter it? And are these the only criteria? What about content as it relates to character, to ethics, to daily life skills and habits of mind essential to succeed *as a person*? What about the academic skills needed to do the core academic work of reading, writing, producing, computing, and thinking? Writing in *Educational Leadership*, Denis Doyle (2003) describes curriculum as "a comprehensive statement describing what students should know and be able to do in order to earn a diploma. Because the curriculum defines what is important and what is not, it is appropriate for each generation to debate what to include and what to exclude" (96). Such remarks raise a question: What roles *are* schools supposed to play in the lives of children today? Some speak of a sacred trinity: school, family, and church; such people usually go on to explain that this trinity is now shattered and that the only part left standing is the school, which must assume the role of instructing students in the content that was once the domain of parents and the church. It goes without saying that not all people agree with this conception of the school; few, however, would disagree with the importance of the content needed to function in today's (and tomorrow's) demanding, rapidly changing society. Instead, they debate *who* should teach the lessons and *how* students best learn such lessons.

Whatever the content of our courses, or a school's curriculum, it should have certain traits. Doyle addresses this in the same article in which he argues for a uniform curriculum (within a school and across a district): intellectual coherence, continuity, and consistency (96). To these I would add that the content must be engaging, meaningful, challenging, and useful. It must meet kids' needs as students as well as employees, citizens, and parents. A curriculum's content should include academic as well as intellectual, moral as well as social, personal as well as practical knowledge and skills. Furthermore, to the extent that such national tests as the New SAT, Advanced Placement exams, and various state tests (e.g., exit exams) align themselves with what is (supposed to be) taught in the classroom, the content of the courses should prepare students for these tests, doing so by embedding the test-prep material within the more meaningful content of the course to prevent it from becoming a mere test-prep course.

One parent, lamenting the demands the prescribed content (i.e., classes, AP, SAT, ACT) made on his son, who was not a fully engaged student, worried that the content of school and its importance to colleges would overshadow his son's other passions, which said much more about the content of his character than his SAT or ACT scores ever would:

> Grades and SAT scores remain the key criteria for college acceptance, even though some institutions say they want "the whole person." . . . But did I mention [my son's] out-of-school life—martial arts training, teaching and youth leadership work and in-depth involvement in a youth performance group? . . . Or the splendid summer between his junior and senior year when he took a master class in hip-hop in Philadelphia, visited the Tule Lake internment camp site, and joined street protestors at the Los Angeles Democratic Convention, using art and performance pieces? Those are the kinds of activities the SAT can't measure, but they are a greater reflection of who our son is and will be. (Wong 2001)

Wong's comments remind us that we are what we study. In his book *Intellectual Character*, Ron Ritchhart (2002) addresses this issue: "The fact is that most schools today do not try to teach for intelligence. Rather than working to change who students are as thinkers and learners, schools for the most part work merely to fill them up with knowledge. . . . When one considers the current emphasis on high-stakes testing and accountability, a more apt description of the mission of schools might be this: to promote the short-term retention of discrete and arcane bits of knowledge and skills. If you think this is too pessimistic a view, take a look at a current high school history, geography, science, or math exam" (7). Others, Hirsch (1988) foremost among them, argue that it is the lack of these discrete facts and other essential background information that undermines students' performance, rendering them "culturally illiterate." Hirsch explains his position in *Cultural Literacy*:

> Literate culture is the most democratic culture in our land: it excludes nobody; it cuts across generations and social groups and classes; it is not usually one's first culture, but it should be everyone's second, existing as it does

beyond the narrow spheres of family, neighborhood, and region. As the universal second culture, literate culture has become the common currency for social and economic exchange in our democracy, and the only available ticket to citizenship. Getting one's membership card is not tied to class or race. Membership is automatic if one learned the background information and the linguistic conventions that are needed to read, write, and speak effectively. Although everyone is literate in some local, regional, or ethnic culture, the connection between mainstream culture and the national written language justifies calling mainstream culture *the* basic culture of the nation. (22)

Hirsch argues that certain content knowledge is a means of entering and succeeding in not only the country called School but the one called America also. The domains of knowledge students must learn, and which schools are increasingly held responsible for, include:

• *Academic:* Discipline- or subject-specific knowledge such as students learn through the study of literature, mathematics, science, social science, health, and the arts. Includes an understanding of the people, events, trends, language, and concepts needed to study these subjects. While this necessarily includes those skills appropriate to each subject area, the emphasis in this chapter is on the knowledge, not the skills, needed to succeed in each academic course. Skills are the focus of Chapter 5. It's worth noting that the content of any academic course should include both the conceptual and the practical; thus, in the Economics class, kids would learn about not only the history and framework of the banking system but how to use the system (e.g., open and maintain a checking account; obtain and manage a credit card account).

• *Social:* Knowledge of other people, customs, and the conventions that govern social interaction between students and those (i.e., peers and adults) with whom they work during the course of their day. Social content includes manners and appropriate behavior in a range of different situations. Of all of Ron Clark's "essential 55" rules (2003) for academic and personal success, manners and respect rank at the top.

• *Procedural:* The knowledge of how and when to use certain tools (e.g., a computer), resources (e.g., the Internet), facilities (e.g., the library), and processes (e.g., the writing process).

• *Cognitive:* Self-knowledge of the mind and the processes used to learn, remember, and solve problems. These habits of mind constitute those aspects of our mental processing (e.g., memory recall, meaning making, problem solving as it applies to tasks in each discipline) needed to succeed.

- *Cultural:* Understanding of different cultures and customs used in reading, writing, and speaking. Includes not only cultural reference points (e.g., important events or people) but values and ideas that are often expressed through proverbs, idioms, and symbols.

- *Vocational:* Familiarity with a wide range of ways of living and working in the world. Includes not just types of jobs but the knowledge and values related to working; these inevitably overlap with the other domains mentioned here. Such knowledge extends beyond an understanding of different fields of work to include an examination of the requirements (e.g., education) needed to enter into and succeed in a given domain.

- *Ethical:* Recognition of certain situations as ethical dilemmas that require an understanding of how to make ethical decisions. All subject areas in the curriculum come with complex ethical content; such content offers teachers some of the most engaging material and powerful opportunities for learning. This content also includes a clear and effective understanding of plagiarism and cheating.

- *Existential:* School prepares students not just for work but for living; thus, a complete education would include an ongoing discussion of what constitutes a good life and how the content of any course will help students achieve such a happy life.

Clearly not all of these domains are listed on states' content standards. While some, such as the academic standards, are nonnegotiable and subject to measurement, others appear on this list simply to recognize that they have a place at the table of each students' education. They also recognize the vast challenges teachers face as they try to weave this content into a coherent, comprehensible, and useful body of knowledge that students can use in a variety of situations both in and outside of school.

The best way to understand what academic content includes is to look at university requirements, teachers' review sheets, final exams, and, of course, state standards. Here, for example, is a list of the University of California's required courses for entry into the four-year university:

History/Social Science (2 years required)
- American government
- Modern world history
- U.S. history

English (4 years required)

Mathematics (3 years required, 4 recommended)
- Algebra
- Geometry
- Calculus

Laboratory Science (2 years required, 3 recommended)
- Biology
- Chemistry
- Physics

Language Other than English (2 years required, 3 recommended)

Visual and Performing Arts

Elective (1 year required)
- Applied physics
- Economics
- Journalism
- Marine biology
- Psychology
- Speech

(Source: San Mateo Union High School District "UC-Approved Course List" for 2003–04)

"New Standards" (Tucker and Codding 1998) offers a more national perspective on academic content. These performance standards "are derived from the national content standards developed by professional organizations" (255). Their standards are organized as follows:

English Language Arts
1. Reading
2. Writing
3. Speaking, listening, and viewing
4. Conventions, grammar, and usage of the English language
5. Literature
6. Public documents (high school level only)
7. Functional documents (high school level only)

Mathematics
1. Number and operation concepts
2. Geometry and measurement concepts
3. Function and algebra concepts

4. Problem solving and mathematical reasoning
5. Mathematical skills and tools
6. Mathematical communication
7. Putting mathematics to work

Science
1. Physical sciences concepts
2. Life sciences concepts
3. Earth and space sciences concepts
4. Scientific connections and applications
5. Scientific thinking
6. Scientific tools and technologies
7. Scientific communication
8. Scientific investigation

Applied Learning
1. Problem solving
2. Communication tools and techniques
3. Information tools and techniques
4. Learning and self-management tools and techniques
5. Tools and techniques for working with others

(255)

A more detailed examination of content—taken, in these examples, from high school history and biology classes—appears on review sheets for chapter and final exams. Here are two representative examples, the first from a review sheet for a modern world history class chapter exam:

CHAPTERS 25, 26, AND 27 TEST REVIEW

Industrial Revolution	factors of production	external forces
crop rotation	proletariat	David Livingston
Jethro Tull	Friedrich Engels	Cecil Rhodes
industrialization	communism	King Leopold II
entrepreneur	unions	quinine
textile factories	collective bargaining	racism
Liverpool-Manchester Railroad	Jane Addams	Shaka Zulu
James Watt	The Reform Bill of 1832	European motives
middle class	suffrage	The Great Trek
enclosures	Queen Victoria	internal forces
	psychology	urbanization

child labor
Alexis de Tocqueville
laissez-faire
corporation
socialism
Adam Smith
capitalism
Thomas Malthus
Karl Marx
utilitarianism
bourgeoisie
The Communist
    Manifesto
Anglo-Persian Oil
    Company
Pacific Rim
British East India
    Company
Emiliano Aguinaldo
jewel of the crown
Queen Liliuokalani
The Third Republic

anti-Semitism
Zionism
Thomas Edison
Alexander Graham
    Bell
Henry Ford
assembly line
The Wright Brothers
mass culture
Louis Pasteur
Joseph Lister
theory of evolution
radioactivity
Social Darwinism
Sepoy Mutiny
Southeast Asia
Ram Mohun Roy
Charles Darwin
King Mongkut
Ivan Pavlov
annexation
assimilation

Maxim gun
Royal Niger
    Company
Berlin conference
The Ottoman Empire
Boer War
Selim II
paternalism
The Crimean War
Nigeria
Suez Canal
Menelik II
tobacco boycott
Suleiman I
sepoys
geopolitics
colonialism
Muhammed Ali
Raj
The Belgian Congo
French Indochina
imperialism

ESSAY QUESTIONS: Be prepared to answer *one* of the following questions:

1. Discuss the economic, social, and political effects of the Industrial
   Revolution.
2. Choose two of the inventions, discoveries, or new ideas that occurred
   between 1700–1900 and describe them in detail. Identify who was responsible for it and how it affected people's lives.
3. Identify at least two (2) causes and two (2) effects of European Imperialism
   between 1750 and 1900.

   Here is an end-of-the-semester review sheet for a biology course:

Expect the following topic areas to be included in the final exam:

UNIT 1: BIOSKILLS
1. Measuring techniques (length, mass, volume, temperature)
2. The correct use of the microscope (including parts and functions)
3. Microscope measuring techniques

4. Metric conversions (the decimal ladder will be provided)
5. Reading and interpreting tables and graphs

UNIT 2: ECOLOGY
1. Food chains and webs
2. Pyramids: energy, biomass, population
3. Cycles: CO_2, N_2

UNIT 3: CHEMISTRY
1. Inorganic chemistry
    a. Atomic structure (electron, proton, neutron configuration given the periodic table)
    b. Matter: molecules, compounds, mixtures, solutions, solute, solvent, concentration (gradient)
    c. Ionic bonds: acids and bases (pH scale) and salts
    d. Covalent bonds
    e. Hydrogen bonds
    f. Characteristics of water (polar molecule, hydrogen bonds, surface tension, capillary action, adhesion, cohesion)
2. Organic chemistry
    a. Polymers and monomers of carbohydrates, proteins, lipids, and nucleic acids
    b. Carbohydrates (monosaccharides, disaccharides, polysaccharides)
        1. Examples and functions
        2. Be able to identify the molecular and structural formula for glucose
    c. Proteins (peptides, polypeptides)
        1. Examples and functions
        2. Be able to identify the structural formula for an amino acid
        3. Functions of proteins as enzymes (i.e., catalase)
    d. Lipids
        1. Examples (i.e., fats, waxes, oils, greases)
        2. Be able to identify the structural formula for glycerol
        3. Be able to distinguish between the structural formulas for a saturated and unsaturated fatty acid
    e. Nucleic acids (also see Unit 7)
        1. Examples (DNA, RNA)
        2. Structural components (nucleotides)
        3. Functions

UNIT 4: THE CELL

1. Distinguish between eukaryotes and prokaryotes
2. Parts and functions of the cell
3. Distinguish between plant and animal cells

UNIT 5: IN AND OUT OF CELLS

1. Cell membrane structure
2. Passive (osmosis, diffusion, facilitated diffusion) and active transport
3. Predict how a plant and animal cell will behave in a hypertonic, hypotonic, and isotonic solution

UNIT 6: ENERGY

1. ATP–ADP cycle
2. Photosynthesis input and output in:
   a. Light reactions (photo system I and II)
   b. Calvin cycle
3. Cellular respiration (ATP production):
   a. Glycolysis
      1. Anaerobic—fermentation (ethanol or lactate production)
      2. Aerobic—leading to the Krebs cycle and electron transport system
   b. Krebs cycle—input and output
      1. Electron transport system (oxidative phosphorylation)—input and output

UNIT 7: DNA

1. Monomers comprising nucleic acids—guanine, cytosine, adenanine, thymine, uracil (in RNA)
2. DNA and RNA structure
3. DNA replication
4. Overview of protein synthesis (transcription and translation)

A more programmatic view of content, one specifically designed to prepare students for success as both people and students, comes from the Talent Development High School Program of the Johns Hopkins University Center for Research on the Education of Students Placed at Risk (CRESPAR) and the AVID program. Here is an overview of the Johns Hopkins Talent Development High School (with Career Academies) program and its content in 2003.

The Essential Tools and Life Skills for the High School Student Freshman Seminar Units

Too many students enter comprehensive high schools without the necessary knowledge of what will be expected of them socially and academically as they move through the high school curriculum toward graduation. Teachers often say that students come to them in high school not knowing how to take notes, or study, or organize their time, or work positively with peers and adults, but those same teachers rarely have the time or opportunity to meet these needs.

FRESHMAN SEMINAR is a new course offered during the first semester of ninth grade, designed to remedy these problems. In-depth lessons that use a variety of both innovative and traditional teaching techniques, including long-term projects, cooperative teaming activities and reflective journal writing, are used in Freshman Seminar to help students practice the study, note-taking, time management, social and human relations skills they need every day in their major academic subjects and in their "real" lives outside of school, as they prepare to choose a Career Academy.

UNIT 1: HIGH SCHOOL ORIENTATION (7 LESSONS)
- Classroom Rules: Getting to Know You
- School Rules: Getting to Know Your School
- Your Notebook: Getting and Staying Organized
- Freshman Seminar Goals
- Middle School vs. High School
- Introduction to Teaming
- Teaming Practice

UNIT 2: STUDY SKILLS (18 LESSONS)
- Introduction to Note-Taking: The Cornell Method, Shorthand, Graphic Organizers, Mind Maps and Classic Outlining
- Memory Principles and Mnemonic Devices
- Previewing and SQ3R
- Time Management
- Study Space
- Test Preparation
- Test Anxiety

- Taking Objective Tests
- Taking Essay Tests

UNIT 3: CAREERS (13 LESSONS)
- Introduction to Careers
- The Holland Inventory
- The Holland Codes
- Investigating Careers
- Lifestyle, Occupation, and Education
- Writing a Resume
- The Job Application
- The Job Interview

UNIT 4: COLLEGE (10 LESSONS)
- Types of Colleges: Lifestyles and Careers
- The Tests You'll Need to Take
- Different Kinds of Colleges
- Choosing a Major
- College and Income
- College Costs and Financial Aid
- Reading a Transcript
- Alternatives to College

UNIT 5: HUMAN RELATIONS (15 LESSONS)
- Dynamics of Conflict
- Conflict Loops
- Approaches to Conflict
- Problem Solving
- Understanding Our Emotions
- Strategies for Controlling Anger
- Active Listening/I-Messages
- Coping with Being Left Out
- Resisting Peer Pressure
- Dealing with Disrespect
- Dealing with Authority
- Solving Conflicts with Parents and Teachers
- Making Good Choices

Content

UNIT 6: TECHNOLOGY AND RESEARCH (15 LESSONS)

- Basic Keyboarding
- Introduction to the Internet and the Research Process
- Simple PowerPoint Presentations

UNIT 7: COMPLETING A LONG-TERM PROJECT: CAREERS REVISITED (15 LESSONS)

- Writing the Career-Centered Essay
- Peer Editing of Student Writing
- The Interviewing Process
- Post-Graduation Pathways
- Career Academies
- Writing Note Cards
- Career Presentations

UNIT 8: SOCIAL SKILLS (13 FIVE-PART SKILL ACTIVITIES)

- Brainstorming
- Cooperation
- Active Listening
- Staying on Task
- Keeping Self-Control
- Disagreeing Without Being Disagreeable: Challenging Ideas, Not People
- Asking for Clarification/Help
- Helping Someone
- Compromising
- Remaining Calm Under Pressure
- Staying Out of Trouble with Peers
- Settling Differences Without Fights
- Taking Turns/Giving Everyone a Fair Chance

While these different examples of formal content represent what counts, all classrooms are subject to other types of content, which, in some cases, define the culture of the classroom and thus directly influence the context in which students learn the primary content. What are these other types of content? They include content that is often not directly taught but which is nonetheless easily felt, heard, and seen in the classroom environment and interactions. Such invisible content includes teachers' (and other students') attitudes toward concepts and students themselves. Through various remarks or the teacher's tone, students receive implied content; the teacher's editorial comments on the value or credibility of certain subjects or ideas makes an impression on the students, especially if students respect that teacher. As Ted Sizer and Nancy Faust Sizer (1999) write, "The students are watching. How we adults live and work together provides a lesson. How a school functions insistently teaches" (116). Thus, we, the teachers, as well as our behavior, our biases, and our ideas, are an inherent part of the content; we bring to our classrooms all our assumptions, experiences, values, and knowledge, all of which influence not only what we teach but how and why. Some teachers endeavor to make the curriculum itself and the process by which it is created an essential part of the course's content; they challenge students to ask why they read and study what they do, urging them to consider what voices are *not* part of the course's content, what ideas are not included, what assumptions the teachers, writers, or society makes about them as students, as readers, as people.

In the end, if content is to matter, is to be effective, it must connect to not only who we are but who we are trying to become. It must serve, as Carol Jago (2001) says, as both a mirror and a window, showing us who we are and who we could be, even as it develops in us the knowledge and skills needed to become that person. Above all, we must remember, as the poet W. B. Yeats told us, that "education is not the filling of a vessel but the lighting of a fire." So it is for the teachers: we are not only the kindlers of such fires but the custodians of these fires as well as our own. Surely no one became a teacher to dispense facts; rather, we fell in love with the content of a field about which we care deeply, and we must endeavor to inspire in our students a similar love.

What Factors Affect Content?

Even if content were neutral, the process of delivering it is not. Whatever we teach passes through too many hands to stay clean. Between editors and teachers, writers and state education officials, the content comes to students preprocessed. While I already mentioned some factors that affect content, it is worth looking more closely at what shapes the content we teach so we might better prepare ourselves and, more importantly, the students to be wary but intelligent consumers of content. A list of factors might include:

- Ethos of the content
- Purpose or context of the content

- Commitment and competencies related to the content
- Teacher's knowledge of the subject
- Students' culture, experiences, and background knowledge
- Means of instruction

Ethos refers to power and credibility; in most cases, it is used to describe people—a speaker, for instance—but in this case I apply it to the content itself *as well as* the teacher and the texts used to deliver the content. Several key factors contribute to the ethos of the content in the classes students take and the lessons they learn. First would be the importance of the content. While similar to relevance, importance here means the significance of the material as it relates not only to the student but to the society. A second, related aspect of ethos is the usefulness of the content. Ours is, after all, a practical country, one in which we routinely ask why we need to learn something; underneath such questions is the issue of usefulness. The obvious and routine example is the student who struggles in algebra and wonders aloud what he will ever do with algebra. Another aspect of ethos is the degree of difficulty, the extent to which the content engages the students' minds with real challenges that create both a context for learning and the opportunity to show what they know and have learned in the current situation. The fourth component of content ethos involves the quality of the content students encounter. Quality in this case refers to the authenticity, accuracy, depth, and credibility of the course content. When students receive antiquated textbooks in poor condition, they are right to assume the content will be worth less than that available to kids at schools with the latest materials. Indeed, such inadequate materials compromise the integrity of not only the class or the teacher but the school itself. In *Moral Questions in the Classroom: How to Get Kids to Think Deeply About Real Life and Their Schoolwork*, Katherine Simon identifies three related features of a "well-functioning, intellectually focused course":

- Pedagogical coherence (order)
- Intellectual honesty (depth)
- Critical reflection (use of evidence and alternate interpretations) (2001, 37)

Another factor that profoundly affects content and students' response to it is the context and purpose of that content. A perfect example would be a potentially engaging text that is used instead to prepare students for a state exam. Students want to engage in a discussion about difficult choices inspired by a piece of literature, for example, but chewing through the same story to prepare them for a state test is not a compelling purpose unless the student is desperate to pass the test and the content offers an apparently useful means of achieving that end. Other contexts are situational. While cheating is not a formal part of my course content, it quickly becomes content when a student cheats; for instance, one time I discovered that a student's paper was copied from a website and offered as her own. This decision created a context for an urgent and consequential discussion of ethics, which became a much more important part of the course content than her essay on the novel we had finished and about which she had "written." On another occasion, a student in my ACCESS program announced that he would be leaving four days before Winter Break to go skiing with his friend's family. "But Ryan, there are only two weeks left of the semester. You will miss the big exam in history. You've worked so hard to overcome your earlier failure." I pressed him on this for some time that day, getting him to see the consequences of his decision, how it would affect teachers' perspectives on him and their commitment to his success. When he walked into class the next day with a grin on his face (instead of a scowl), I knew he had grown up a bit the night before; when I asked him about it, he said he realized taking the trip was not the right thing to do. Thus my class' life content was more pressing in that context than any academic content.

Still other factors have an impact on the content. Teachers' knowledge of the content directly contributes to the credibility and general ethos of the content. Some content flies in the face of community standards, which deem certain subjects inappropriate. Such community standards, as well as those imposed by the state and district, can, in some cases, undermine the teacher's professional integrity, taking from them the intellectual and pedagogical control they need if they are to feel invested in and committed to what they teach. Without such a vested interest, teachers become little more than fast-food servants feeding the students information. Students themselves, along with their culture, experiences, and general background knowledge, exert a powerful influence on the content of the course. Taking *Huck Finn* into an urban school with a large African American student population would be a different experience than teaching it in a suburban high school; a still different experience would come from a school of mostly English learners (sometimes called a newcomer school) who were asked to read *Huck Finn*, a book that would no doubt leave them a bit perplexed about our language and how they should speak.

This last example leads to one final factor, one whose importance is as evident as it is crucial: the means of instruction, which is to say *how* the teacher teaches the *what* (i.e., the content). After studying math teachers in Japan, Germany, and the United States, researchers conducting the Third International Math and Science Study (TIMSS) drew the following conclusions about effective instruction:

- *The goal of the lesson.* Strong lessons were more likely to target mathematical thinking while weak ones were narrower in goal, seeking to teach students how to solve a particular kind of problem or carry out a specific procedure.

- *Treatment of mathematical concepts.* In strong lessons, the concepts were far more likely to have been developed rather than simply presented as rules.

- *Multiple lesson strategies.* Strong lessons included multiple ways to solve problems.

- *Strong lessons were focused and coherent.* Weaker ones switched topics significantly more times.

- *Strong lessons included mathematical reasoning.* Whether this was formal proof or informal reasoning, mathematical reasoning was explicit.

- *Complexity.* The complexity of tasks within a strong lesson was likely to increase.

- *Type of problems.* Strong lessons generally asked students to perform tasks that were not "routine." That is, they weren't plain calculations or problems for which students just applied a formula that was given to them. In strong lessons, students might have to figure out which formula to use or find more than one way to solve the problem.

- *Connections.* In strong lessons, teachers helped students make explicit connections between parts of the lesson to previous knowledge, and/or to statements and problems from earlier parts of the lesson. (Stigler and Hiebert 1999)

This summary of insights into mathematics instruction could just as easily be about any other subject; certainly as a high school English teacher, I find it useful when thinking about, creating, or evaluating my own curriculum and instructional methods. Others (Langer 2002; Applebee 1996; Marzano 2001; Stevenson and Stigler 1992) offer different but related insights into those instructional methods that help students not only learn but understand and remember content. Langer (2002) found six features common in schools that "beat the odds" with students who do not typically succeed in school or perform well on standardized tests. These six features are:

1. Students learn skills and knowledge in multiple lesson types.
2. Teachers integrate test preparation into instruction.
3. Teachers make connections across instruction, curriculum, and life.
4. Students learn strategies for doing the work.
5. Students are expected to be generative thinkers.
6. Classrooms foster cognitive collaboration.

Langer says elsewhere that effective literacy instruction in middle and high school has other traits:

1. **It is dialogic.**
   - Classroom talk is an extended discussion in which comments build upon one another.
   - Students and teacher share and debate interpretations of texts.
   - The teacher poses or gets the students to pose authentic questions.
   - The teacher introduces strategies for generating understanding.
   - The teacher provides support for all students to participate in reading, writing, and discussion.
2. **Activities are designed to support students' developing envisionments.**
   - All students are expected to have interesting and relevant ideas, questions, hunches, and understandings.
   - Multiple perspectives are treated as ways to enrich understandings.
   - Students explain and defend their points of view using supporting evidence in texts and their own experiences.
   - Teachers support envisionment building by insuring students develop effective strategies for developing understanding and for participating.
3. **The curriculum is structured around extended curricular conversations.**
   - Conversations are around key issues or ideas that provide direction and continuity.
   - Conversations adhere to a variety of ground rules about how arguments are formulated and evidence presented.
4. **Academic demands are high for all students.**
   - The topics and tasks in which students are engaged require significant investments of time and mental energy. (2003, 4)

In *The Learning Gap* (1992), Stevenson and Stigler emphasize the following characteristics of effective instruction. They say successful students:

- Have a teacher who leads them to make discoveries that underlie further acquisition of knowledge and to make generalizations to other material;
- Are presented with lessons that are well scripted and well organized, and that use multiple approaches to illustrating the principles or ideas being taught;
- Are given an idea of why they are learning certain material, and the material is presented in a context with which they have had some experience;
- Are given frequent opportunities during the course of learning to interact with other children in generating ideas, explaining answers, and evaluating the adequacy of their own and other children's answers;
- Are provided with clear information about the relevance and accuracy of their answers, and are not made wary of trying new ideas because mistakes are interpreted as failure;
- Have hands-on experience with the material being discussed, and have the opportunity to see how the principles are derived before they are discussed in abstract terms or are formalized;
- Are presented with multiple examples of a concept so that they can deduce the underlying principle, and are required to come up with some of the steps toward the solution themselves;
- Are provided with opportunities to practice what they have been taught.

Carol Ann Tomlinson (1999) emphasizes the importance of providing access to challenging content through differentiated instruction. She identifies several principles for effective differentiation of instruction:

1. The teacher is clear about what matters in subject matter.
2. The teacher understands, appreciates, and builds upon student differences.
3. Assessment and instruction are inseparable.
4. The teacher adjusts content, process, and product in response to student readiness, interests, and learning profile.
5. All students participate in respectful work.
6. Students and teachers are collaborators in learning.
7. Goals of a differentiated classroom are maximum growth and individual success.
8. Flexibility is the hallmark of a differentiated classroom.

Each of these lists represents the complex nature of content, as well as the multiple sources of that content; it comes from everywhere, is subject to multiple influences, and requires effective instruction if students are to learn, understand, and remember it. These scholars' findings also reiterate the central role of teachers' own content knowledge about not just their subject but effective instruction, the world outside of school, and the kids themselves. "The classroom teachers are [after all] the ultimate arbiters of what is taught, and how. Regardless of what a state policy requires or what a district curriculum spells out, the classroom teacher ultimately decides how much time to allocate to particular school subjects, what topics to cover, when and in what order, and to what standards of achievement, and to which students. Collectively, teachers' decisions, and their implementation, define the content of instruction" (Wisconsin Center for Education Research 2002). Marzano provides perhaps the most useful perspective on instruction and content, one that synthesizes much of what this section has addressed. Comparing the curriculum to a spiral, Marzano (2001) suggests, "The fundamental principle underlying the concept of a spiral curriculum is that students should be introduced to new knowledge in its most rudimentary form. During subsequent encounters with the knowledge, however, more skill and depth of understanding should be expected" (109). Marzano outlines that progression of increasingly complex learning in his taxonomy (see Figure 1.2). He concludes his remarks by noting that instructional "strategies that focus on metacognitive and self-system processes" had some of the most profound effects on student achievement.

Returning to the opening example of the AP English teacher and her concern about students' lack of knowledge, I will close with a brief update that illustrates much of what I have discussed so far. By the end of that first meeting, when teachers' scores on the sample AP exam ranged along a continuum, we realized the truth of the AP teacher's claim. Clearly the kids were not learning much because we all needed to know more ourselves. We committed ourselves to studying poetry throughout the year so as to increase our own knowledge of this genre, its conventions, the poems themselves, and how to teach them. We invested in resources that would help us achieve that good (*The Making of a Poem: A Norton Anthology of Poetic Forms,* by Mark Strand and Eavan Boland) and designated a specific and reasonable time to meet (the collaboration day we had once a month for an hour). And when we met, we discussed not only the poems and what they meant but *how* they meant it and how we might go about teaching it. We found shelter in one another's company in the small room where one day a month we gathered around the table, around the text, to warm ourselves at the fire of our colleagues' minds, helping one another become the teachers we want to be by learning what we needed to know to accomplish that. In the process we learned, we laughed, and we left the hour feeling what I can only describe as—content.

FIVE
Competencies

Young people can no longer count on a predictable future

and cannot expect that a set of skills learned in school

will be sufficient to ensure a comfortable career.

—Mihaly Csikszentmihalyi and Barbara Schneider,
*Becoming Adult: How Teenagers Prepare
for the World of Work*

COMPETENCIES are those skills students need to be able to complete the
assignment or succeed at some task.

Representative, general academic **competencies** include the ability to:

Communicate ideas and information to complete and convey results of the work.

Evaluate and *make decisions* based on information needed to complete the assignment or
succeed at the task.

Generate ideas, solutions, and interpretations that will lead to the successful completion
of the task.

Learn while completing the assignment so students can improve their performance on
similar assignments in the future.

Manage resources (time, people, and materials) needed to complete the task; refers also
to the ability to govern oneself.

Teach others how to complete certain tasks and understand key concepts.

Use a range of tools and strategies to solve the problems they encounter.

After dropping out of high school, my father entered the printing business, where he learned skills that any able-bodied seventeen-year-old could easily master: cutting, taping, aligning, and calculating. It was a variation on assembly line work: images arrived on his desk, which he then had to photograph and lay out, preparing them for placement in a book that then went to a second line of workers: printers. If you were willing to work, you could learn the skills and get the job done. When he was getting ready to retire thirty-eight years later, my father hired only people who knew how to use advanced publishing software like PageMaker. Those whose skills had not grown with the onset of the digital era were forced to retire or accept lower-paying jobs at the printing plant.

Men and women in these new jobs made decisions no one would have trusted my father with in the old days; the laborer my father had been had evolved into a combination of designer, publisher, and production manager. This transformation from being part of the machinery to using such advanced machinery to complete a range of sophisticated tasks is the same one Miles Myers describes in his book *Changing Our Minds: Negotiating English and Literacy* (1996): "Why were these new skills needed? The need for these new skills grew out of, among other things, the new technology" (9). Such changes in the workplace and the skills demanded of more and more adults in America created a need for what economist Robert Reich (1992) calls the "symbolic analyst"; if workers didn't make this transition, they were likely to be replaced by "smart machines" (Zuboff 1989). Reich explains: "Budding symbolic analysts learn to read, write, and do calculations of course, but such basic skills are developed and focused in particular ways. They often accumulate a large number of facts along the way, yet these facts are not central to their education; they will live their adult lives in a world in which most facts learned years before (even including some historical ones) will have changed or have been reinterpreted. In any event, whatever data they need will be available to them at the touch of a computer key" (1992, 229). Myers and Reich, among others, raise the question Just what *are* the essential competencies our students will need to succeed in the world for which we are preparing them? And is it the job of the school to develop such skills, or is our purpose to teach them how to learn so when they reach the next level—in a university or at a company—they know how to learn what people are teaching them?

Judging by a Public Agenda poll (see Figure 1.1), professors and employers are not happy with the skills current students possess. The Public Agenda findings highlight what all adults know and many kids who struggle in school resist: adults judge one another according to what they can do and how well they do it. Such public performances, what Tom Newkirk (1997) calls a "performance of self," express our public identity, defining us in the eyes of others as competent or incompetent people, who sometimes develop their skills to the level of craftsmanship. Such personal investment in one's work, however, can come only from doing work that matters, that means something to the people doing it. In *An Ethic of Excellence: Building a Culture of Craftsmanship with Students*, Ron Berger (2003) writes,

> The first step in encouraging high-quality student work is to have assignments that inspire and challenge students. . . . [At my school] projects are the primary framework through which skills and understandings are learned. They are not extensions of the curriculum or extras when the required work is done. They are themselves at the core of the curriculum. In the course of a thematic study there may be three or four significant projects, most of which require research, writing skills, drafting skills, and sometimes mathematical or scientific skills. In the course of these projects there are usually traditional skill lessons and traditional informational lectures as in any school. The difference is that these skills are put to immediate use in the service of an original project with high student investment. (67)

Returning to basketball coach John Wooden's Pyramid of Success, note that Wooden places skill at the center of the pyramid, saying in essence that without the essential competencies, all the commitment, content, and capacity in the world won't save you when it comes down to the competition of the real world. American universities appear to share this conviction, for numerous recent reports (e.g., Conley 2003; Intersegmental Committee of Academic Senates 2002) focus on the centrality of skills needed to succeed in challenging college-level courses: "Understanding and mastery of . . . content knowledge . . . is achieved through the exercise of broader cognitive skills. It is not enough to simply know something; the learner must possess the ability to do something with that knowledge, whether it is to solve a problem, reach a conclusion or present a point of view. This plexus of content knowledge and cognitive skills is what an education at an American research university (and many other institutions of higher learning) seeks to develop" (Conley 2003, 9).

In light of the challenges students will inevitably face in the future, researchers now speak of "habits of mind" (Costa and Ballick 2000) or "Megaskills" (Rich 1997), which serve as a set of intellectual tools students can use in a variety of situations over the course of their lives. As Mihaly Csikszentmihalyi and Barbara Schneider (2000) write, "The difficulty in teaching young people relevant occupational skills is that, to a degree unprecedented in American history, nobody quite knows what these skills [of the future] might be" (17). Some, of course, think they know exactly what these skills will be. In *Teaching the New Basic Skills: Principles for Educating Children to Thrive in a Changing Economy*, the authors identify six "new basic skills":

- The ability to read at the ninth-grade level or higher
- The ability to do math at the ninth-grade level or higher
- The ability to solve semistructured problems where hypotheses must be formed and tested
- The ability to work in groups of persons of various backgrounds
- The ability to communicate effectively, both orally and in writing
- The ability to use personal computers to carry out simple tasks like word processing (Murnane and Levy 1996, 32)

Competencies: What They Are

The competencies needed to excel in a subject (e.g., algebra) are not the same skills that translate into overall academic success as a student. As Mooney and Cole (2000) explain in their book *Learning Outside the Lines: Two Ivy League Students with Learning Disabilities and ADHD Give You the Tools for Academic Success and Educational Revolution*: "We discovered no one had ever really given us skills for academic success and personal empowerment. We had at our disposal only skills that had been developed by professors and teachers that were detached from the reality of being a student. Many of these skills were punitive; they tried to fix us and fit us more into some impossible model. Ultimately, all of these skills were based on the idea of one type of mind and one way to learn, and in the end were simply not good ways for us to learn" (81).

After examining the school skills of successful students for a couple of years—so I could teach my ACCESS students how to achieve similar success—I developed the following summary of school skills, which we take time to discuss in some detail over the course of the first month of school. They are not the typical core academic competencies we assess on state tests; rather, they are the skills that translate into success in school and, in many cases, the workplace later on. They include:

Decisions   Every day, in each class, you must make decisions that have important consequences. You decide *if* you will pay attention, get to class on time, or do an assignment. If you decide to do the assignment for that class, you must then decide if you will do your best or not. If the assignment is difficult, you must decide if you will persevere—or quit. Successful students make decisions based on priorities and goals.

Allies
Schools are filled with people who will help you. Each student needs to find the allies that best meet their needs. Some allies help you solve personal or social problems; others, usually teachers, help you work through the academic problems you face and guide you toward the success that you seek. Allies are people you give permission to teach you about not only math, for example, but life also. Nearly all successful students seek out and create relationships with one or two adults at school who support, guide, even push the student to do their best.

Permission
Successful students give *themselves* permission to try, to learn, to listen, to admit that they need help, and to seek help from those who can teach them. They give *teachers* permission to help them, to teach them, to challenge them.

Academic Behavior
Successful students talk to teachers with respect. They understand that politeness matters. They use the teacher's name: "Miss Reyes, I'm not sure I understood that. Could you please go over it one more time? Thank you." They greet the teacher and/or say good-bye. Other important behaviors that contribute to a positive academic identity include nodding or otherwise showing that you are listening; asking questions (to clarify, to show you're listening, to participate), sitting up straight, having only the appropriate books and supplies on your desk. Makeup, candy, money, gadgets, or backpacks on your desk suggest that you do not care—about this class, the ideas, or your future.

Organization
Successful students are organized. They use a planner to keep track of what they have done and need to do. Their planner is full of information, notes, reminders. They bring their planner to every class; as soon as the teacher says, "For homework, . . ." the successful student opens their planner and writes down the homework. They organize time so they get work done—and have time for fun. They think ahead. The teachers note this behavior; it shows that the student takes the class and the teacher seriously.

First Impressions	Because people make decisions about others based on first impressions, it is essential to make the right first impression. Not only *what* you say but *how* you say it contributes to the teacher's (and your classmates') impression of you. How you handle the first assignment will further add to the teacher's expectations: If your work shows commitment, they will take you seriously as a student. If you go to them for help, they will think you care, that you are making the extra effort to succeed—and they will respect you for it. How you dress, your manners, your overall attitude—these significantly affect the teacher's impression. If, for example, you come to class the first day and do not have a pen or paper and slump down in your desk and won't look at or respond to the teacher, the teacher will quickly assume you do not want to be taken seriously as a student and will soon come to expect less of you if your future actions reinforce the first day's impression.
Supplies	Invest in supplies and have plenty of extras on hand so you don't run out or have to ask others. Asking others for supplies you should have suggests you are not committed to your work and the class. It also disrupts the class and distracts other students.

ALL CLASSES	SCIENCE/MATH
• Binder(s)	• Graph paper
• *Plenty* of binder paper	• Compass
• Pens, pencils, highlighters	• Protractor
• Hole punch	
• Good dictionary and thesaurus	
• Planner/organizer	
• Required texts and materials	
• Student ID card	
• Calculator (ask your teacher which type)	

Grades	When it comes to grades, one important question to ask is simply, "What counts?" It's also important to realize that just because something isn't graded right away doesn't mean it

doesn't count. It's essential that you do *all* assignments. Consider this example of grade trouble: A student gets two A– grades (90/100) on exams and doesn't take the third. Their grade in the class? 90 + 90 + 0 = 180/300 (60% or D–). Here is a representative breakdown of grades for most classes, though this example comes from a math class:

Participation/attendance:	10%
Tests:	40%
Quizzes/warm-ups:	20%
Homework:	15%
Groupwork/projects:	15%

Attendance

Be in class, on time, and ready to work. Anything less undermines your chances for success. If you are absent, classmates lose faith in you and don't want to work with you on projects. Also, you get behind on assignments, even as you receive new ones that must be done by tomorrow. You can quickly get buried beneath a mountain of work you feel you can never complete. If you are tardy, you lose points, especially if your teacher begins the class with an immediate warm-up activity or quiz that you cannot make up. Principals often *encourage* teachers to begin class with such activities as an incentive for being on time, and a punishment if you are not. When you are absent—or know you will be—approach the teacher and tell them you are sorry you missed class and are eager to make up the work. If you know you will be out for more than one day, call the school and ask them to inform your teachers so they can submit assignments to the office, which someone can bring home to you (which keeps you from getting behind). Again, this shows that you are committed to doing well in school.

Participation

Participate in class, around school, and in the community at large. All these activities contribute to success in school and life. People who participate consistently report that they enjoy school, saying that they feel they are benefiting from all the school has to offer. In class, participation means asking questions, contributing to class discussions, *doing* whatever is going on. Around school, participation means joining clubs, running for student government, going out for teams, and performing in plays or with the school band. It might also mean participating in a community service activity like teaching senior citizens how to use computers, cleaning up the local beach, or reading to kindergartners. Some classes—yearbook, newspaper, public speaking, leadership—offer unique opportunities to participate in the life of the school. The more you give (in class, around school, within the community), the more you get.

Help   Successful people ask for help. The best students in the class might look like they know it all, but what they really know is that it's okay to ask for help when they need it. So when you don't understand, ask the teacher to clarify: "Mr. Harris, I'm not sure I understand what you just said, could you go over that again, please? Thank you." Or approach the teacher after class and ask when you can meet to discuss your paper, an exam, or some assignment that is giving you trouble. They will not be annoyed; they'll be *impressed!* They will see a young adult who is committed and wants to be taken seriously.

Requirements   *Graduation:* What you need to accomplish depends on what choices you want to have when you graduate. Successful students always know where they stand in relationship to graduation and their long-term goals. Here is an example of the graduation requirements:

English	40
Math	30
Physical Education	20
Science	20
Social Science	30
Foreign Lang/VisPerform Arts/VocEd	20
Health	5
Elective	55
Required Minimum Credits	**220**

Note: One semester course = 5 credits (e.g., English: 40 units = 4 years of English)

> *Eligibility:* Students must maintain a 2.0 GPA in order to participate in athletics, spirit squad, student government, and musical/dramatic performances.

Balance: ASEP

School smarts involves more than just academic success. Some people ignore all other aspects of their life to achieve success, usually at a great cost in terms of health, fun, and relationships. Balancing the different areas of your life is essential if you are to succeed. ASEP stands for the four key areas of need: academic, social, extracurricular activities, and personal. You must concentrate on and invest in your *academic* success, but you must also ensure that you have a *social* life, that you get out and have fun. *Extracurricular activities* such as those discussed here under Participation are also important; they provide rich opportunities, new relationships, and a feeling of belonging to the school community. Finally, tending to *personal* needs—hobbies, church, health, family—is crucial if you are to maintain your overall health and happiness.

Success

Smart students know that success is not something easily attained and must be repeatedly earned over the course of the year. Success is an attitude, a value, a way of life. While many have their theories about what leads to success, I favor Tom Morris' Seven Cs of Success. Morris argues that to succeed (and maintain that success), we need:

1. A clear **conception** of what we want, a vivid vision, a goal clearly imagined.
2. A strong **confidence** that we can attain that goal.
3. A focused **concentration** on what it takes to reach the goal.
4. A stubborn **consistency** in pursuing our vision.
5. An emotional **commitment** to the importance of what we're doing.
6. A good **character** to guide us and keep us on a proper course.
7. A **capacity to enjoy** the process along the way.

One could, of course, argue that many of these are not skills. Yet woven throughout these school smarts are such skills as managing resources, negotiating, evaluating, organizing, collaborating, motivating, and solving problems common to academic work in all classes. One colleague found her current kids' "student skills" so lacking she mentioned them in her annual Christmas letter: "Teaching itself has been more challenging than usual. This year's crop of 9th graders is more challenging than I am used to, not necessarily behavior problems or even individuals with poor literacy skills. The problem is, alas, their lack of student skills. They don't bring binders, books, pencils to class, and homework seems to be a nasty germ that many of the students try their best not to catch. I am trying new spins . . ." (LePell 2003). Aside from her insight into the source of students' troubles, this teacher embodies Morris' third C because she responds to students' lack of skills by reflecting on and improving her own in order to teach them how to be successful students.

It's much easier to understand what school smarts include and what they look like in action by hearing what a student says about them. Reflecting on his freshman year from the safe shore of June, Cameron Harris, a young man who learned more about the world and himself in a year than most will learn in ten because of some important experiences he had, offers such a perspective in this letter written as part of his final portfolio:

Dear Prospective Reader:

This year I have altered relatively every aspect of myself as a student and a person. I am a completely different person and student than I was at the beginning of the year, and an even more diverse person than I was last year.

As a reader, last year I pretty much began at square one. I hated reading and never did it, even when I was assigned to do it. As that year progressed, I began doing the assigned readings and pondering reading outside the class. As this year began, I read in the class, as well as outside the class. However, therein lay one problem—I really did not understand my purpose while reading. It seemed as if I was reading just to "get it done," and I did not get a chance to enjoy the texts. When this school year commenced, I was introduced to a brand new style of reading. I now knew what to do while I read. As the year progressed, I delved deeper and deeper into various aspects of the book that I had never even thought of before. I read to look for answers to questions I had developed beforehand. I read to relate the book to the world and to my life, and most of all I now read for enjoyment and the need to feed my longstanding hunger for knowledge.

I had always thought that writing had to come from the world around you and the things that you already knew. I had succeeded relatively well under this assumption to some level of course. In the years past, I had never thought to look inside myself to derive my ideas, and to write my own inner emotions and feelings down on paper. Prior to this year, I had found writing to be a laborious chore that I attempted to complete as quickly as I could. I have learned that writing is a very positive way to get my feelings out and reflect on myself and the world. I learned to "teach" myself to be a better person from writing and reflecting on what I wrote and how it relates to the world around me. From doing this I learned to be more perceptive and appreciative of others and the subtle world in which I live. I also learned how to respect others and myself. Writing this year has helped me grow as a student and most of all as a person.

I have always been accustomed to *two* different forms of thinking. One for when I was around others and thinking for school, and the other when I pondered life alone. While I was in school and around others, I had the mentality of "black and white" thinking. I thought in common terms, either something was or it wasn't. I guess I was just scared to share my feelings with others for the fear of rejection or embarrassment. However, when I began ninth grade, and as the year went on, I gained a tremendous amount of confidence and felt much better about myself. I became more comfortable with my thoughts and believed that others would like to hear them. I realized that motivating discussions could be derived from my comments. I began to think out loud as often as possible, and my writing and my personality have both grown from that.

Public speaking has always been one of those things I wasn't afraid of, but I resented. When I ran for class office in 6th through 8th grade, I felt comfortable in front of everyone, but I dreaded every moment leading up to "the big moment." I began to enjoy spreading my opinions to others, and what better way to do so than aloud, the more people that can hear the better. I have improved my speaking skills through simulations such as "The Golding Trial" and the "South Africa Simulation." I feel public speaking will prove to be a great asset later on in my life's journey.

Through all of these improvements and the assignments that went along with them, I have learned to NEVER procrastinate. Doing work in advance takes much of the stress off of your shoulders, and who needs the extra stress? I know I certainly don't. My non-procrastination has led me to compose much better work at a much more comfortable pace.

Perseverance and hard work, these are the goals that I will concentrate on next year. I must concentrate on both of these if I am to succeed. These goals are very important because it is the absence of these things that almost led to my downfall this year. When things seemed bad and unlucky I sort of "quit." The world around me was beginning to fall apart, and I felt as if there was no point to working anymore. I let up and the quality of my work dropped. I was so caught up in feeling sorry for myself and concentrating on the past that I forgot who I was. I AM NOT A QUITTER. There are a lot of things that I am, but a quitter would be the absolute last. I have never quit anything that I cared for in my entire life, and I was beginning to do just that. With my allies standing behind me, I jumped back on the right track. Next year, that will not happen. If I maintain perseverance throughout the year, the outcome will be most favorable. No matter how many obstacles are hurled my way, and no matter how bad things seem, I will keep pushing on because that is who I am. It just took me awhile to find who I am, and I am still finding that out. That will be another one of my goals—to find who I truly am and apply that knowledge to my studies and my relationship with myself and others. If I accomplish these goals, I will succeed and I will do great things.

Sincerely,
Cameron Harris

Cameron's letter offers a powerful portrait of not just academic but personal success, both of which will clearly lead to adult success. Throughout his letter he notes the different aspects of academic success, some of which he had, some of which he learned. Of course, most find such a set of academic competencies too abstract and not applicable to the adult world of work. To speak of "habits of mind," "Megaskills," or the five "human passions" (Costa and Garmston 2001) is to ignore the core intellectual skills students need to conduct research, write papers, solve mathematical problems, read sophisticated texts, and take exams. Yet some skills are arguably common to all classes. Such a list might include:

1. Locate information
   - Find and evaluate primary and secondary sources
   - Collect data and make measurements
2. Analyze information to find structure
   - Relative and absolute chronologies
   - Cause-and-effect
   - Classification into hierarchies of categories
   - Compare-and-contrast
   - Main ideas and subordinate supporting detail
3. Create a variety of representations of information
   - Visual
     - Graphical organizers, maps, charts, graphs, diagrams
   - Textual
     - Reports, summaries, outlines
   - Numerical
     - Tables

- Symbolic
  - Functions, literary forms
- Multi-modal
- Models, posters, presentations
4. Make contextual connections
   - Between artifacts and the times (context) in which they were created
   - Between one's own experiences and the artifacts created by others
5. Pose and answer questions
   - Distinguish artifact and contributor, avoiding personal attacks
   - Use appropriate register and language
6. Move beyond what's given
   - Draw inferences or conclusions
   - Make generalizations
   - Make predictions
7. Support a point of view
   - State a thesis
   - Offer supporting arguments
   - Offer logic or evidence
8. Use a problem-solving process
   - Read unfamiliar terms and build vocabulary
   - Develop testable hypothesis, collect data, affirm or disprove hypothesis
   - Brainstorm, outline, create multiple drafts
   - Design or use simulations to explore behaviors and relationships
   - Use functions to generalize dependencies, create a model, etc.
   - Identify a problem, gather information, list and consider options, decide on and implement a solution, and evaluate the results
9. Reflect on processes and products (artifacts)
   - Participate in collective reflection on class or group activities and artifacts
   - Engage in reflective abstraction from one's own experiences and concepts
10. Demonstrate the use of conventions and mechanics of the English language
    - Adjust language and tone to accommodate conversational norms
    - Adjust grammar and vocabulary to fit the audience
11. Demonstrate degree of mastery in formative and summative assessments
    - Accept objective, valid feedback or criticism as formative
    - Use assessment to develop plans for action (Springer 2003)

The academic essentials I emphasize and teach in my own classes are required for success in any academic course; we learn how to:

- Read
- Write
- Talk
- Skim and scan
- Summarize
- Analyze
- Ask questions
- Take effective notes
- Take tests

After spending a year sitting in college classes and examining what the professors expected students to be able to do, Mike Rose (1989) arrived at his own set of core academic competencies:

- Define
- Summarize
- Serialize
- Classify
- Compare
- Analyze

Rose writes: "I finally decided to build a writing curriculum on four of the intellectual strategies my education had helped me develop—some of which, I would later discover, were as old as Aristotle—strategies that kept emerging as I reflected on the life of the undergraduate: summarizing, classifying, comparing, and analyzing" (138). After further reflection, he added the other two: defining and serializing. Only by mastering these skills could Rose's students enter what he calls "the academic club" (141), which Frank Smith has dubbed "the literacy club" (1988). Comparing students to travelers and school to a foreign country, Rose goes on to say, "A traveler in a foreign land best learns names of people and places, how to express ideas, ways to carry on a conversation by moving around in the culture, participating as fully as he can, making mistakes, saying things half-right, blushing, then being encouraged by a friendly native speaker to try again" (1989, 142).

Figure 1.3 shows my own version; these academic literacies came from a range of sources, but mostly they derive from a decade of working with high school freshmen and identifying the traits of effective students. A more succinct list of "student competencies" (Fielding, Schoenbach, and Jordan 2003) is shown in Figure 5.1.

Over the last few years I have kept lists of different skill sets outlined in various books and articles. The following examples are representative and suggest different perspectives on the notion of competencies as they relate to not only school but the workplace and civic life. Robert Reich (1992), former secretary of labor under President Clinton, offers these skills in his book *The Work of Nations*, dividing them into the three types of work he foresees will be done in the future:

ROUTINE PRODUCTION SERVICES (30%)
- Repetitive tasks
- Work with many other people doing the same thing, in large enclosed spaces
- Guided by standard procedures and codified rules, and over-seers
- Wages based either on time or amount of work
- Must be able to read and to perform simple computations
- Cardinal virtues: reliability, loyalty, and capacity to take direction; standard American education (K–12) will suffice

IN-PERSON SERVICES (30% AND GROWING FAST)
- Simple and repetitive tasks
- Wages based on hours worked or amount of work
- Closely supervised
- Need not have acquired much education
- Provided person-to-person
- Work alone or in small teams
- Cardinal virtues: punctual, reliable, tractable; must smile, exude confidence and good cheer—even when they feel morose; must be courteous and helpful, even to the most obnoxious of patrons. Above all, they must make others feel happy and at ease

SYMBOLIC ANALYSTS (20%)
- Essential skills: problem-solving, problem-identifying, and strategy-brokering activities
- Symbolic analysts solve, identify, and broker problems by manipulating symbols. They simplify reality into abstract images that can be rearranged,

ACADEMIC LITERACY STUDENT COMPETENCIES

AREA OF COMPETENCY	EXAMPLES OF WHAT STUDENTS WILL KNOW AND BE ABLE TO DO
Personal Dimension	• Become increasingly aware of preferences, habits, processes, and growth as readers • Set goals for purposeful engagement with reading • Increase reading fluency • Increase confidence, risk taking, focus, and persistence in reading
Social Dimension	• Share confusions about texts with others • Share successful processes and approaches to understanding texts with others • Participate in small- and large-group discussions about reading and texts • Appreciate alternative points of view
Cognitive Dimension	• Monitor comprehension • Ask different types of questions of the text • Summarize the text • Clarify understanding of the text by rereading, searching for context clues, continuing to read, and tolerating uncertainty • Make predictions based on the content or structure of the text
Knowledge-Building Dimension: Content	• Use a variety of strategies to access and interpret information in textbooks and other course materials • Preread texts and generate questions • Use graphic organizers to organize and build knowledge structures • Identify and access relevant knowledge and experiences
Knowledge-Building Dimension: Texts	• Identify text features such as signal words and specialized vocabulary • Approach novel words strategically, using prior experience, context, and structural clues to meaning • Identify and use structural signal words and phrases
Knowledge-Building Dimension: Disciplines and Discourses	• Recognize the large questions, purposes, and habits of mind that characterize specific academic disciplines • View texts as constructed artifacts that are addressed to readers familiar with the worlds they represent • Become familiar with specialized vocabulary, semantics, concepts, phrases, idioms of different disciplines and discourses
Writing	• Write from a particular point of view • Respond to text excerpts • Paraphrase texts • Compose a variety of texts for different purposes (interviews, reflections, summaries, letters, descriptions, logs, commercials, journals, posters, oral presentations)
Research	• Categorize, synthesize, and organize information from texts • Evaluate information sources • Identify primary and secondary sources • Interpret primary source documents

FIGURE 5.1. Academic Literacy Student Competencies. "Apprenticeship Model"; an updated version can be found in *Building Academic Literacy: Lessons from Reading Apprenticeship Classrooms, 6–12* by Ruth Schoenbach. Reprinted by permission of the author.

juggled, experimented with, communicated to other specialists, and then, eventually, transformed back into reality
- Rarely come into direct contact with the ultimate beneficiaries of their work
- Often have partners or associates rather than bosses or supervisors
- Income depends on the quality, originality, cleverness, and, occasionally, speed with which they solve, identify, or broker new problems
- Careers are not linear or hierarchical
- May take on vast responsibilities and command inordinate wealth at rather young ages
- May lose authority and income if they are no longer able to innovate by building on their cumulative experience
- Often work alone or in small teams, which may be connected to larger organizations, including worldwide webs
- Teamwork is often critical
- Since neither problems nor solutions can be defined in advance, frequent and informal conversations help ensure that insights and discoveries are put to their best uses and subjected to quick, critical evaluation
- When not conversing with their teammates, symbolic analysts sit before computer terminals—examining words and numbers, moving them, altering them, trying out new words and numbers, formulating and testing hypotheses, designing or strategizing
- Bulk of the time and cost (and, thus, real value) comes in conceptualizing the problem, devising a solution, and planning its execution
- Most graduate from four-year colleges or universities; many have graduate degrees as well

Thomas Friedman's vision for the global society and the skills needed to succeed in it challenges us to think deeply about which competencies our school curriculum develops. In *The Lexus and the Olive Tree: Understanding Globalization* (1992), Thomas Friedman suggests that to be successful in a global economy, people must acquire the ability to:

Manage
- Relationships (both personal and professional)
- Personal and professional needs
- Resources, assets, information
- The present in light of the past and the future
- Complexity

Communicate

- Using multiple and appropriate means (e.g., multimedia, images, words, numbers, different languages) to convey the information or message to a range of people with different concerns or needs

Teach

- Others and yourself using those means—i.e., tools, techniques, methods— which are most effective for learning this skill, idea, or job

Learn

- Quickly
- By multiple means: example, manual, experience; written, spoken, demonstrated instruction
- From yourself as much and as easily as from others

Observe

- Patterns of behavior (of people, markets, processes)

Decide

- Using appropriate information from multiple reliable sources in different domains
- How to approach a problem and why that is the best approach in this situation

Imagine

- The past
- Other possibilities
- Other perspectives
- The future

Organize

- Information
- Resources
- Time
- Processes
- People, including yourself

Respond

- To situations
- To information about performance of products, ourselves, or markets
- To changes
- In a timely, appropriate, and effective manner

Design
- Experiences
- Products
- Processes
- Networks
- Systems

Evaluate
- Quality of information with regards to veracity, reliability, credibility, applicability
- Possible purposes to which certain information can and should be put
- Performance (of people, product, market, process) in light of expectations, standards, or criteria
- According to personal, ethical, cultural, political, economic, and other principles

Search
- For information, people, products, or ideas using a variety of tools and techniques

Represent
- Information, ideas, and processes using language—words, symbols, images, sound—to ensure that all people understand what you mean

Create
- Opportunities
- Products
- Meaning
- Community

Work
- Efficiently
- Independently
- Collaboratively
- Creatively
- Hard
- Fast

Persuade
- People using stories, numbers, facts, images, and ideas, to see your side, adopt your perspective, act in accordance with your message, believe what you say

Identify
- Essential information and ideas
- Stages in a process
- Elements (the parts from which the whole is made)
- Patterns and their implications
- Relationships, especially cause-effect

Such skills make the more fundamental skills such as "writing an effective paragraph" or "using a variety of sentence patterns" seem small. But Reich himself illustrates what students compete against as they endeavor to make a place for themselves not just in the class or school but in the society at large:

> The formal education of the budding symbolic analyst follows a common pattern. Some of these young people attend elite private schools, followed by the most selective universities and prestigious graduate schools; a majority spend childhood within high quality suburban public schools where they are tracked through advanced courses in the company of other similarly fortunate symbolic-analytic offspring, and thence to good four-year colleges. But their experiences are similar: Their parents are interested and involved in their education. Their teachers and professors are attentive to their academic needs. They have access to state-of-the-art science laboratories, interactive computers and video systems in the classroom, language laboratories, and high-tech school libraries. Their classes are relatively small; their peers are intellectually stimulating. Their parents take them to museums and cultural events, expose them to foreign travel, and give them music lessons. At home are educational books, educational toys, educational videotapes, microscopes, telescopes, and personal computers replete with the latest educational software. Should the children fall behind in their studies, they are delivered to private tutors. Should they develop a physical ailment that impedes their learning, they immediately receive good medical care. (1992, 227)

While such opportunities and resources certainly contribute to success, a strong work ethic and investment in the development of necessary skills goes a long way to compensate for the lack of such privileges. As Csikszentmihalyi and Schneider (2000) found in their study of teenagers' attitudes toward work in school and the future, "We see that it is possible, even for notoriously skeptical teenagers, to develop positive attitudes toward the productive side of their lives. What is more those who do so apparently enjoy their lives more and are happier. They have a more purposeful view of the years ahead, and they seem to find personal fulfillment in their work. The youngsters who have developed this positive work ethic are not primarily the offspring of rich and educated parents;

on the contrary, poor and socially marginal youth are overrepresented in this group" (94).

When it comes to competencies, teachers live in the crosshairs of parents and the public: teachers are supposed to prepare students for not only what is to come but what they are to *be*come after they graduate, even if that future is a world that no one can really imagine. One thing is certain: when they leave our classes, our schools, students need to have a suitcase heavy with the skills they need to live in the world, to solve the personal and professional problems that are an inevitable part of modern life. I once knew a teacher who got tired of her own kids saying "Nothing" or "I dunno" (or just shrugging) when she asked them at dinner what they learned in school that day. She began standing at the door each day as her own students left, handing each one a little strip of paper, and saying to each as they left, "Now when you go home tonight and your parents ask you what you learned today in Mrs. Kramer's class, you can tell them you learned how to write adjective clauses [or whatever the lesson of the day addressed]." I like to imagine those slips of paper as tickets to the future. When students arrive in that mythical place called the future, they just want to be ready so they can be as successful as their teachers dreamt they would be so they can come back (or send an e-mail!) someday to say thanks for what those teachers taught them to *do*.

What Factors Affect Competencies?

Why do we find that sometimes we, or our students, are not that competent at a task we have already demonstrated our ability to do reasonably well? My ACCESS class, for example, grew out of a related experience: students in my developmental reading class improved their reading skills but not their grades in academic classes. I soon realized that they had developed a set of general reading skills and had improved their capacity (speed, stamina, and memory) but lacked the specific competencies they needed to tackle unique or increasingly complex demands of text.

Both teachers and students move along a continuum of performance, depending on a range of factors, some of which affect a person's competence in one situation more than another. Figure 5.2 offers a visual explanation of this continuum of performance, which relates not only to students' competence but the teachers' also as they try to teach new material or use new techniques.

As the example of my colleagues and the AP test in the previous chapter illustrates, being an expert (or at least a competent performer) in one area does

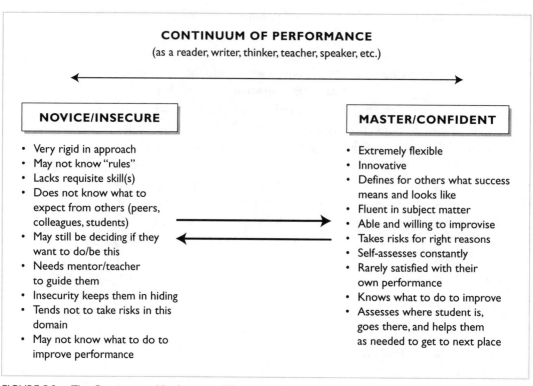

CONTINUUM OF PERFORMANCE
(as a reader, writer, thinker, teacher, speaker, etc.)

NOVICE/INSECURE

- Very rigid in approach
- May not know "rules"
- Lacks requisite skill(s)
- Does not know what to expect from others (peers, colleagues, students)
- May still be deciding if they want to do/be this
- Needs mentor/teacher to guide them
- Insecurity keeps them in hiding
- Tends not to take risks in this domain
- May not know what to do to improve performance

MASTER/CONFIDENT

- Extremely flexible
- Innovative
- Defines for others what success means and looks like
- Fluent in subject matter
- Able and willing to improvise
- Takes risks for right reasons
- Self-assesses constantly
- Rarely satisfied with their own performance
- Knows what to do to improve
- Assesses where student is, goes there, and helps them as needed to get to next place

FIGURE 5.2. The Continuum of Performance. We continually move back and forth along this continuum as we learn and, over time, improve. From *The English Teacher's Companion*, Second Edition (© Burke 2003).

not mean you have the same status in other domains. Despite their skills as literary readers, my colleagues' skills lay mostly in reading fiction; a challenging poem by Elizabeth Bishop slid most of us back along the continuum to various places, some even approaching novice. It's worth noting that their skills in one area (fiction) would doubtless accelerate their learning and performance in another (poetry), especially if one of their other skills was knowing how to learn things they find difficult.

Several other factors affect students' ability to use or improve their competencies in certain areas. These include:

- Opportunity
- Assessment (type, quality, frequency)
- Effectiveness of instruction

- Motivation (includes patience and resilience; confidence; connection to current and future identities as they relate to work and living)
- Cognitive and physical development

Opportunity and available resources play a key role in learning and improving upon skills. Such opportunities include the availability and quality of role models, for students (and teachers) need opportunities to see what competent performances look like in different contexts. Students from successful families are typically enrolled in activities after school and during the summer months that provide structured, effective opportunities to learn and improve upon skills that lead to an identity of themselves as a competent person in one or more domains. As Csikszentmihalyi and Schneider (2000) write in *Becoming Adult*, "More advantaged youth—those from Caucasian backgrounds who live in affluent communities and whose parents are highly educated—will know how to find internships, specialized training, summer employment, and other opportunities to begin practicing the skills of the occupation to which they aspire. They will be helped by the network of knowledge and contacts that constitutes the 'cultural capital' of their family and social class" (63). The authors add another important angle on the issue of such opportunities: personal agency. They note that "personal agency makes a great difference within each environment" (79), for "a housecleaner's child, as well as the child of a wealthy surgeon, can learn to see work as an opportunity to enjoy doing his or her best in an activity that will be important to his or her future" (87).

All the opportunity in the world will do little to improve their skills if students do not get the feedback and guidance they need to become more competent. Thus, another factor that influences the acquisition and improvement of essential academic competencies is assessment. Improvement depends on effective and regular information about what one does well and needs to improve; it goes still further: it provides insight into *how* that individual achieves success and *why* they are not succeeding in other areas. This feedback typically comes from multiple sources in various forms, but it is always timely and specific. Affluent people hire tutors, experts, and coaches to provide such specific feedback about performance in areas such as writing, reading, doing math, taking tests, or general learning skills. As we discussed in Chapter 3, students who come from homes without such intellectual and financial resources must seek out and rely on the commitment of others, usually teachers, to provide such guidance, to become their academic mentors.

Such mentors and guides offer another important benefit that can profoundly affect the student's learning of specific skills: effective, individualized instruction that complements the student's learning, thinking, or working style. It is beyond the scope of this book to examine the specifics of this topic, for it is vast. It is, however, of profound importance and central to much of the current discussion about closing the achievement gap. Mel Levine, author of *A Mind at a Time* (2002) and *The Myth of Laziness* (2003), stresses the importance of each mind's ways of working. Mooney and Cole, in *Learning Outside the Lines* (2000), repeat their mantra of "your mind your way" throughout their book, emphasizing that the key to their success was to be able to learn the material in the way that made sense to them and, when possible, to demonstrate that knowledge in alternative ways such as through interviews instead of essays. In his many books, Howard Gardner argues that students should have multiple "entry points" into whatever they learn and, when possible, the opportunity to use those "intelligences" that help them learn and demonstrate best what they know. Magdelene Lampert's teaching embodies many of these ideas as she talks about providing students with "multiple entry points" en route to preparing for "public performances" of their knowledge as they develop the skills and confidence needed to "become a person who could make sense of mathematics and initiate working on it in the company of [their] peers in school" (2001, 286). Stigler and Hiebert (1999) stress the importance of showing students a number of different ways to solve the same problem. Tomlinson (1999) argues for the use of "differentiated instruction" to meet students' different needs to help them understand the same material and complete the same tasks, even if at different levels of performance. And Marzano identifies nine essential instructional methods in his book *Classroom Instruction That Works* (Marzano, Pickering, and Pollack 2001), basing his findings on extensive research of both classrooms and the literature. In a class of thirty-five it is, of course, difficult for the teacher to play these many roles, though inevitably some do, usually with those students who seek out help, who show what Csikzentmihalyi and Schneider (2000) called "personal agency" (87). Throughout the study of successful students, advocacy on behalf of oneself is a recurring theme; such students will almost inevitably succeed as adults.

Another factor that affects the mastery of certain skills is readiness. Students' cognitive and physical development proceed at different rates. Certainly those in enriched environments are likely to have experiences or opportunities that accelerate that growth. Perhaps most important here is the question teachers must ask when they see students struggling to learn or apply new abilities:

What are the possible explanations for the student's current performance difficulties? They may be emotional or situational; they might also have to do with a lack of content knowledge or commitment. They may also stem from developmental constraints that prevent the student from achieving the desired level of performance *at that time*. Boys, for example, typically run about two years behind girls in development until about their junior year of high school. Commitment, both the student's and the teacher's, is crucial as they muster the resiliency to work through material or tasks that initially elude their grasp.

Motivation to acquire or refine skills merits close attention, for it suggests a change in perspective toward the self, the present, and the future. One frequent rationale for such programs as school-to-work and service learning is that they help students connect to the future work they have realized they want to do. Thus they get focused, take school more seriously, develop those skills needed to succeed in that field. In my ACCESS program, speakers visit on most Fridays. During their talks these speakers frequently refer to the moment when they figured out what they wanted to do, what they wanted to be. What comes through when you listen to them is a sense of revelation: they realized who they were or wanted to be. Soon after this epiphany comes the realization that they must know and be able to do many things to succeed in that domain. So the professional sports announcer told us about honing his speaking skills in his bedroom on an old tape recorder. As he improved, he took the recorder with him to the San Francisco Giants games when he was still a teenager. Buying a cheap seat in a remote part of the stadium, he would do an actual play-by-play of the game there at Candlestick, then go home and evaluate his performance from the recorder, making notes about what he needed to improve. The coordinator of the county recycling program "hated math" in high school but discovered a passionate interest in the environment and engineering; combining those two interests led to college and a string of math classes, one of which she took three times until she mastered the analytical skills needed to become the type of engineer she wanted to be (and her male professors said she would never become).

This issue of identity returns to earlier discussions of the connection between what students are asked to learn and who they are or want to be. If we conceive of self-education in the literal sense of educating one's *self*, the discussion of necessary competencies must make room for students to both explore different selves and make choices that will allow them to develop the skills (and content knowledge) related to the identity they want to take on.

Many factors affect one's skills. These competencies needed to succeed in school or the workplace are the crux of society's concerns about education.

Competencies—which I have here referred to alternately as skills and abilities—differ from and relate to content in important ways; however, we must keep their differences in mind. Teachers understand the difference between content and competencies better than most, for we realize all too well that expert knowledge of a content area (e.g., mathematics after a thirty-year career as an engineer) has no inherent correlation to the skills needed to effectively teach that content to students. Knowing everything about a subject does not mean you have the ability to teach it to a class of real American teens. Some might point to someone like Jaime Escalante, who came to teaching from a career as a software engineer; the truth, however, is that Escalante had distinguished himself *as a teacher* in Bolivia long before he came to the United States. His genius was not in the content of calculus, which he certainly understood well enough, but in how to teach it and get kids to not just understand but love it. By teaching them the skills they needed to solve the complicated calculus problems, Escalante developed in them the skills they needed to solve the problems we face every day as employees, citizens, parents—as people. Skills *are* teachable, success *is* possible, so long as both teacher and student bring the necessary commitment (to themselves, to each other, to the curriculum), learn the essential content, acquire and master the core skills, and, as we will discuss next, develop the requisite capacities students need to achieve and *sustain* academic success.

SIX
Capacity

We naturally associate democracy ... with freedom of action, but

freedom of action without freed capacity of thought behind it is only chaos.

—John Dewey

First LAW: In every animal ... a more frequent and continuous use

of any organ gradually strengthens, develops and enlarges that organ ...

while the permanent disuse of any organ imperceptibly weakens and

deteriorates it, and progressively diminishes its functional capacity,

until it finally disappears.

—Jean Baptiste Lamarck

CAPACITIES account for the quantifiable aspects of performance; students can have great skills but lack the capacity to fully employ those skills.

Primary **capacities** related to academic performance include:

Confidence in their ideas, methods, skills, and overall abilities related to this task.

Dexterity, which allows students, when needed, to do more than one task at the same time (aka multitasking).

Fluency needed to handle problems or interpret ideas that vary from students' past experience or learning.

Joy one finds in doing the work well and in a way that satisfies that individual's needs.

(continues on p. 108)

Memory, so students can draw on useful background information or store information needed for subsequent tasks included in the assignment.

Resiliency needed to persevere despite initial or periodic obstacles to success on the assignment or performance.

Speed with which students can perform one or more tasks needed to complete the assignment or performance.

Stamina required to maintain the requisite level of performance; includes physical and mental stamina.

Around the time I began this book, I took up cycling. Of course I got a book, too, so I could learn how to approach this goal of improved physical health. It said to make goals, so I did: 100 miles a week seemed reasonable. This was, after all, a Bianchi Eros, a beautiful Italian road bike that was so sleek and fast it would probably just do the riding for me. I quickly revised my goal after I came home from my first twenty-minute ride, lungs terrorized, body sweat-soaked, limbs limp. Still, I was proud and well on my way (I thought) until I looked at the odometer and realized that my first ride was only 2.7 miles. After riding 600 miles and losing 35 pounds, I have come to learn about capacity in visceral, personal ways.

The book I read about cycling also said to set up a log to keep track of my progress. This turned out to be invaluable, for it not only let me see my progress on a daily basis but renewed my commitment daily as I saw the results of my efforts. As with so many things, I began to connect this experience to teaching and learning, wondering what insights it might offer me about my students' efforts to get into academic shape. The first thought that came to mind was SSR (sustained silent reading) in my ACCESS classes. Every day we begin class by reading self-selected books for exactly fifteen minutes; then the students keep track of their performance on their Reading Record (see Figure 6.1) to monitor their progress. The idea for this was simple: the kids need a visual representation of the progress they are (or are not) making so that they, too, see that their efforts make a difference.

Figure 6.1 illustrates several key aspects of capacity. Zaniesha's stamina as a reader improves over time as she reads more in the same period of time. Moreover, her speed also improves as a result of her daily "workouts." What's less obvious but equally important is that she moved onto increasingly complex texts, including poetry, as the semester unfolded, thus demonstrating her increased confidence in her abilities as a reader; this confidence was further bolstered by her subsequent improvement in other classes as a result of her ability

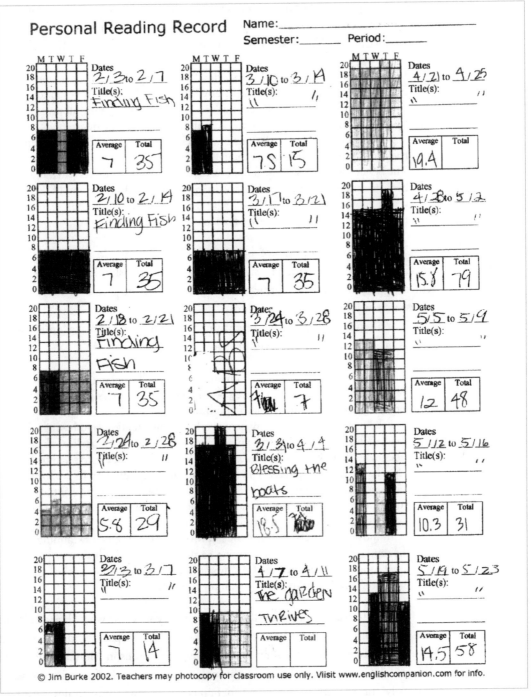

FIGURE 6.1. Zaniesha Woods' Reading Record

to work longer and faster and remember more. Perhaps the most gratifying aspect of Zaniesha's improved capacity is the joy she began to take in reading and succeeding in school. At year's end, she wrote:

> In the beginning of the year I hated school and thought I couldn't get any grades better than C's and D's. As I started this [ACCESS] class I began to grow, not only in my school work but as a person. I started doing all my homework and my classwork to the best of my ability. My grades started improving and then I started gaining more self-confidence. I started becoming friends with people that I never thought I would even give the time of day. The better my grades got the more I realized I should never do less than my best, because if I do then I am just wasting my time. Now at the end of the year, I know that I am the only one who can make my life successful. Not my mom, not my teachers. Me, myself, and I.

These gains in confidence in one area led to confidence in other, more social areas, which demanded a significant capacity for risk tolerance: she joined clubs, did service learning projects, and participated in classes in more public ways such as joining class discussions.

Not all kids find such investment in their intellectual and academic capacity easy to sustain, as Allison Molina shows in her note:

> Beginning this new semester was something I was really looking forward to. A fresh start, an opportunity to make a positive change in my classes, a chance to set new goals, and eventually accomplish them.
>
> I thought that just doing my homework, paying attention, and having good attendance was going to help my grades improve, but I've realized that it takes more than that. It takes dedication, stability, and in some cases, knowledge. In my case, math has been a struggle for me. Already, even in the "new" semester, I have been trying to keep my focus on my work but my wants overpower my needs sometimes. I feel like I basically give up, and it shouldn't be that way. It's just really hard for me sometimes.
>
> In the rest of my classes, I feel the improvement that is kinda swimming to the top, so to speak. I have been trying harder, yet last week I had some personal issues that distracted me for a minute and today, Monday . . . the first day of the week, I am trying to get on my feet again.

It's easy to read a note like Allison's and think you know what she's all about. We must constantly remind ourselves that the students' capacities in one domain do not necessarily apply to other areas. For example, Allison Molina, who failed English and many other classes, rarely spoke in classes, and often missed classes, routinely traveled after school to San Francisco (about twenty miles away) by train, bus, or friend's car to a serious poetry workshop she learned about from one of the ACCESS guest speakers. There, she worked with great care for long hours on her poems, which she eventually performed at open-microphone events on weekends. She got involved, through that group, with a related outreach program called Youth Speaks, while continuing to not only work on her own spoken-word poetry but help others with theirs. Finally, she created WordUp!, a spoken-word community for kids at our high school. I described this briefly in *Teaching with Fire: Poetry That Sustains the Courage to Teach* (Intrator and Scribner 2003):

> Fridays during lunch my classroom fills with kids seeking a place they can call home. Many of these kids, to borrow from Heaney's poem, have suffered, been hurt, turned hard. Heaney writes, "No poem or play or song / Can fully right a wrong / Inflicted and endured," but the kids who come to WordUp! would disagree.
>
> On Fridays these teenagers celebrate themselves, raising their voices in song and verse against the wrongs they've endured. They heal themselves and each other through the water of their words, finding the hope they need to "believe that a further shore is reachable from here," as Heaney says.
>
> I am not the one who heads this gathering; rather it is a quiet girl named Allison Molina, a junior who said simply that kids need a place to "say what they gotta say." On Fridays, I sit quietly in the back of the room eating my lunch, watch the kids shuffle in, and hear Allison call for "respect!" as she convenes the WordUp! with a poem.

Here is a poem that represents Allison's work at around that time, which would hit you all the more if you heard her speak it in her own style and voice:

UNTITLED
By Allison Molina

We
The breed of the outcasts and rebellious teens
Fall behind humanity's modern theories
Of what it means to be successful
Our hands bleed and yearn for the paper
Just to look fly
Just to be liked
Cause nowadays fabrics and nice rides
Seem to symbolize importance
As internal beauty crumbles at the realities of good grades and glamour
Media crazy, most of society absorbs ignorance
Distortion grows
Contagious to all the emerald green source
That disperses greedy trades
In this Babylon disguised under the title of the "United" States

See I've forgotten how it's like
To interact with a society that is intact with unity
Egos have tainted so many souls
So this is where confusion unfolds
Where we stand is where oppression manifests itself
Depression beats and suffocates my consciousness
My eyes see beyond the angles of a rich kid's mind
Yo! We know what it means to struggle
It was a gift that evolved out of time
And I'm searching for a revolution that I will never find
As the fault evaporates at my feet
Due to the fact that I was born to parents that shine shoes
And clean bathrooms just to make ends meet
I'm crying to a higher power, as my knees scar on the floor
Repetition condemns my insistence on this road alone
Pleading for salvation on this microphone
Walking the urban streets
Incomplete
Breaking just to cope with a loss of a shelter that I knew since I was born
Now my fate threw me a fast one
Called a broken home
Yo! Joe Blow . . .
Why must you hate on me?
Is it because my heritage consists of immigrants that come to this country for liberty?
Or cause my main dish is tortillas and refried beans?
But damn homie!
I am flesh and blood just like you!
Your hearts are replaced by a race
Then I guess that's where discrimination comes through
Now you're telling me that cause we lead different lives, we can't associate?
"Upper Class" "Lower Class"
Status only attracts the blind
Those who fail to see the things that really matter in life
God created man equal!
Brothers and sisters, we must unite!
The conclusion to my wishes has become my sacrifice
I've sacrificed just to stay alive
Hope is now slippin' slowly through the grip of my hands
I just want to find love at last
Though it's become a routine for my pride to deteriorate
Amongst the eyes of dishonest men
That will never replace the company of my father that I lost when I was eight
This "love thing" has been gone for so long
And it's so hard to adapt to it
L-O-V-E has been welcomed onto the list of the clichéd

So it hurts to love
As love loves to hurt me
Constantly
Patience sticks with thickness in back of my mind
Cause I want to be loved beyond ages
Breaking restrictions of categories, hairstyles, and artificial differences
Escaping the limitations
Shining transparently through the ironies of all the amendments
Equivalently living
Praying forever for forgiveness
Cause I can't stop sinning
Love erases the elements of thoughts that wrongfully linger
In international infinity.

Later, Dave Yanofsky, director of a youth arts organization, asked Allison and two other ACCESS students to address a group of county school leaders to discuss the importance of the arts for teens. She was a sophomore at this point, and when she returned from the meeting at the county office of education, I wrote her the following note:

Dear Allison,

I wanted to take a minute to say once again how proud I am of what you did Friday (and with your poetry this semester). Below you will see Dave's email to me about how you three did. I wish I could have been there, but am glad I was not for the success seems now all the more your own and the achievement that much more impressive.

Few students have taught me more than you have in the span of the last year and a half. It is a great blessing to be your teacher and I look forward to all we get to learn from each other in the semester (and years) ahead.

Your teacher,
Mr. Burke

Jim,

The meeting went extremely well. Josh, Jeff and Allison made a huge difference—their eloquence in discussing their own poetic inspirations as well as the poetry itself. Whether you intended it or not, they brilliantly represented the diversity of the youth movement, stylistically and personally. The educators in attendance were powerfully moved and one woman even took time out to publicly thank them for coming to the meeting and sharing their words. From my standpoint, it was an important display, proving that young people are gravitating to language in exciting new ways. I can speak till I'm blue in the face, but hearing it directly from the teen poets carries even more weight.

Dave

Allison's story is an important one. It reminds us of the complexity and unseen, private capacities students often have but do not always reveal within our academic settings. Her story illustrates her steady growth of capacity in some areas—confidence, language, joy—even as she struggled in other areas. Eventually her academic failure caught up with her and, in the face of various unpalatable choices, she left our school for a more urban setting, where she felt more at home. There she committed herself to school in a way she had not previously done and, in a powerful demonstration of the Four Cs outlined here, she achieved a success she did not at our school. Here is a note I found slipped under my door some time after I helped her with an essay she had to write at her new school:

Mr. Burke,

Hello there! I came to BHS today specifically to thank you for your help on the essay. I am grateful for every time you've been there to guide me through the obscurity I've faced through these years. I thank you from the deepest corners of my existence! I hope all is prosperous in your realm—continue to touch lives, inspire, and create. You do it well. I hope one day I will be as successful in my life as you have come to be. You are an educator, *that's dope.* Oh yeah, I forgot to mention that . . . I received an *A* on that essay due to your guidance. Take care of yourself and write forever!

Much respect,
Allison Molina

Capacity matters. We all have students in our classes who are committed, have a good grasp of general content, possess well-developed or proficient skills—and lack the speed required to succeed on exams, the memory or dexterity needed to complete certain tasks, the stamina to work through difficult problems, or the confidence to begin work they do not believe they can complete successfully. In a chapter titled "Do Mathematicians Have Different Brains?" Keith Devlin (2000) commented on the capacities needed to do serious work in mathematics, saying, "mathematical thought requires considerable determination and effort—more than almost any other mental pursuit. . . . I am sure that [the determination and effort] are factors that prevent many people from becoming proficient in mathematics. It isn't that they are incapable of intense concentration. Rather, they don't appreciate in advance the degree of concentration required. Hence, instead of giving it that concentration, they assume they just don't have the math gene" (131).

Capacity: What It Is

The different capacities needed to succeed in school become more clear and urgent when we consider the competing demands on students' time, energy, hearts, and minds. Here is a representative list from a focus group of freshmen at my high school who were asked what worried them most in the beginning of high school:

- Making new friends
- Losing old friends
- Harder classes than before
- Seniors picking on/making fun of you
- Final exams
- Homework
- New subjects/information
- Not sure where to go/getting lost
- Missing or being late to class
- Meeting new people
- Peer pressure
- Focusing
- Too many events
- Balancing activities and academics
- Rumors
- Bad influences

Capacities seem to fall into several categories. Judging from this list and previous comments, we might identify the following types of capacity:

- Emotional
- Mental
- Physical
- Social

These general categories might be further broken down to specific capacities such as these:

- Confidence
- Dexterity
- Fluency
- Joy

- Memory
- Resiliency
- Speed
- Stamina
- Tolerance

Speed is the most unjust aspect of academic success. It should not matter how much time a student needs to complete the work so long as that student can do so and thereby meet the standards. The current push to cover so much content in less time is problematic, for it increases the pressure on students to do more in less time; such stress inevitably affects other capacities such as memory, joy, and confidence. Speed is not limited to how quickly one takes a test or reads; it's more useful to think of it as processing speed. Some kids are like the tortoise when it comes to generating ideas, connections, examples; others are out of the gate like the rabbit, filling up their papers with well-rehearsed or easily created assertions and supporting examples. Sometimes their speed slows down because they want to do the work so well; other times they bog down because they do not clearly understand the directions; on still other occasions they may be overwhelmed by all the possibilities they have generated, as in the example that follows.

To prepare my sophomore ACCESS students for the state exit exam essay, we practiced getting out of the gate fast. We rehearsed strategies that would help them take apart the topic and generate ideas. After about ten minutes, without prior warning, I told them to stop and draw a line under what they had done so far. I then asked them to reflect on *how* they had begun, and if they had not yet begun at all, then to explain why. Jorge Rodriguez, who still had a blank page, had anything but a blank mind, as his response shows: "I'm having a hard time getting started because there are so many people who have influenced me throughout my life. These people have influenced me in different ways, so it's hard to pick just one." What's interesting is that once Jorge had this little moment of reflection, he felt free to pick his father, having honored the others in his life, and he then focused on his father:

> Now that I think about it, there is someone who had influenced me the most and that is my dad. The way he has influenced me is to teach me never give up on my dream or to at least have one. My dad's dream was to make it as a professional runner, but he did not get there because he injured his knee. Since he never got there, he wants me to make it big time in soccer and I want to make him proud.

Since we were just practicing openings, this was a pretty dramatic turnaround in only a few minutes. What seemed like a problem with his capacity to generate was actually nothing of the sort; he needed some strategies to help him make more efficient selections from his options, guided in this case by which one he could write about best to pass the exit exam. Mike Rose discussed this same process of learning to master academic language and expression: "I was struggling to express increasingly complex ideas, and I couldn't get the language straight: Words, as in my second sentence on tragedy, piled up like cars in a serial wreck. I was encountering a new language—the language of the academy—and was trying to find my way around it" (1989, 90). Both Langer (2002) and Marzano (2001) emphasize the importance of teaching students to be "generative thinkers" by giving them the strategies to produce hypotheses, solutions, connections, claims, and so on.

Another crucial capacity is stamina. Stamina applies as much to the mind as to the body; it is physical and mental. One area of particular concern to teachers is attention. Mel Levine (1994) compares attention to a symphony conductor "who does not actually create the sounds of music but who controls the players of instruments who in turn generate the actual melodies . . . and 'thinking players,' individual brain processes that are essential for learning, behaving, and relating well to others" (10). Levine further articulates those aspects of attention that affect performance by representing them as "the Concentration Cockpit" (see Figure 6.2).

I have had students in ACCESS use the Concentration Cockpit to assess their capacity; doing so demystifies the notion of attention and helps them realize how much is going on. It's rather like lifting up the hood of a car and realizing how many parts are involved in making it go. I ask students to use the following scale to evaluate themselves in each of the different domains Levine identifies in the cockpit model:

0 = I have a big problem with this.
1 = I have a little problem with this.
2 = I have no problem with this.
3 = I am excellent in this area.

I then have them do some writing and reflecting on what they learned about themselves. Here is one student's response:

When it comes to attention, I do somethings better than others. My sixth period is Athletics, but since I'm on the JV team I get in the pool [for water polo] at 3:30. I do as much homework as I can until I get in. Since there are a

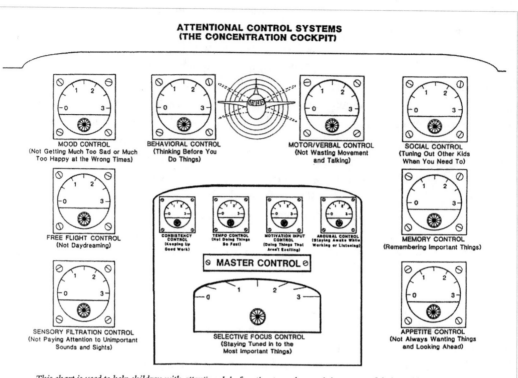

**ATTENTIONAL CONTROL SYSTEMS
(THE CONCENTRATION COCKPIT)**

MOOD CONTROL
(Not Getting Much Too Sad or Much
Too Happy at the Wrong Times)

BEHAVIORAL CONTROL
(Thinking Before You
Do Things)

MOTOR/VERBAL CONTROL
(Not Wasting Movement
and Talking)

SOCIAL CONTROL
(Tuning Out Other Kids
When You Need To)

FREE FLIGHT CONTROL
(Not Daydreaming)

CONSISTENCY
CONTROL
(Keeping Up
Good Work)

TEMPO CONTROL
(Not Doing Things
So Fast)

MOTIVATION INPUT
CONTROL
(Doing Things That
Aren't Exciting)

AROUSAL CONTROL
(Staying Awake While
Working or Listening)

MEMORY CONTROL
(Remembering Important Things)

MASTER CONTROL

SENSORY FILTRATION CONTROL
(Not Paying Attention to Unimportant
Sounds and Sights)

SELECTIVE FOCUS CONTROL
(Staying Tuned In to the
Most Important Things)

APPETITE CONTROL
(Not Always Wanting Things
and Looking Ahead)

This chart is used to help children with attentional dysfunction to understand the nature of their problems. An adult explains each of the controls on the cockpit, and the child draws her or his needle on each dial (0 = I have a big problem with this, 1 = I have a little problem with this, 2 = I have no problem with this, and 3 = I am excellent at this).

FIGURE 6.2.   Mel Levine's Concentration Control Cockpit

lot of people talking, I can't consitrat [*sic*] on my note taking or reading, so I do my math. If I try to read while people are around me making noises I have to reread over and over again. My next problem is probably day dreaming, but I don't do it that much. The only time I do it is when something really exciting happens or is going to happen. I start to think about it in class, but if I really try to consintrate [*sic*] I pay attention. The excellent attention I have is mood control. I like to always be a positive person. I don't like being mad so I tend to be happy. I can't really get mad at life because I love it too much.

After the exit exam one year I had students in my ACCESS class evaluate how their attention, commitment, and confidence changed over the course of the exam, which took all morning. One student's diagram and comments (shown in Figure 6.3) represent the type of challenge many students face when it comes to attention stamina.

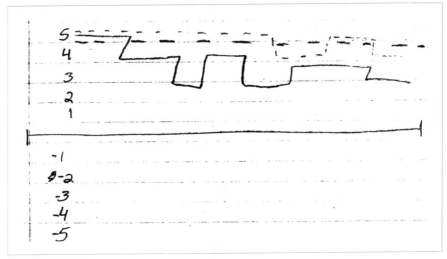

FIGURE 6.3.   I asked kids to represent their performance. The solid lines represent Lourdes' confidence over the course of the exam; the small dotted line represents stamina; the larger (flat) dashed line represents attention.

When asked to explain the diagram, Lourdes Toloza wrote: "I was really focused until the end of the test when I started to think about something else. But in this class there were two girls who were talking and writing notes. That made it really hard to focus." Of particular importance is her comment about the way her attention ran out. If we think of attention as a fuel, we have to help Lourdes learn to conserve the fuel she has so she can achieve greater attention capacity.

What Factors Affect Capacity?

Memory and confidence are two other crucial aspects of capacity. When I first began thinking about the Four Cs, I asked students to evaluate their performance on the state exams (two days of testing in language arts, math, and science) and to explain their diagrams. I should note that this assignment was also part of a larger unit on reading graphics; thus, we looked for ways to represent their content knowledge and develop their competencies in the area of representing information through visual explanations.

Ben Pierce explains his diagram, shown in Figure 6.4, thus:

When it comes to math, I can get it done. English and science is another thing. Math I'm confident about because I've gotten so many A's on so many math tests, while English and science I've gotten so many F's. We all can't do

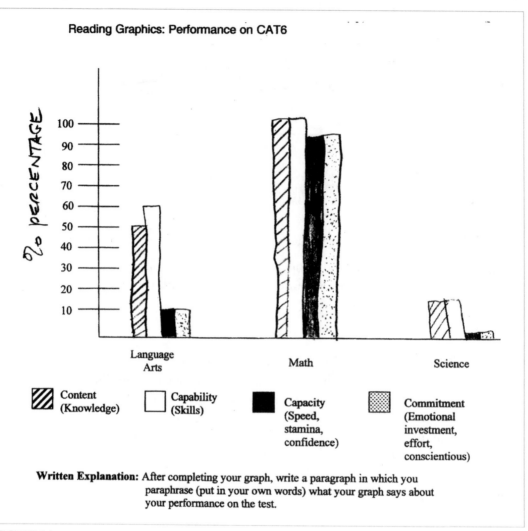

Reading Graphics: Performance on CAT6

% PERCENTAGE

▨ Content (Knowledge)	☐ Capability (Skills)
■ Capacity (Speed, stamina, confidence)	▩ Commitment (Emotional investment, effort, conscientious)

Written Explanation: After completing your graph, write a paragraph in which you paraphrase (put in your own words) what your graph says about your performance on the test.

FIGURE 6.4.

things as well as others, whatever it may be. For me, it's memory. That's it. If I remembered what I learned in science, I would not have done so bad. If I would have remembered to read more at home, I wouldn't have taken so long on the English part of the test. It's all time. Once you have control of your time you can accomplish anything.

Again we hear, as we have in other students' comments about school, the emphasis on confidence. The root of the word is *fide,* which means faith; thus, when we confide in someone, we place our faith in them, for example. When we read the following excerpt from Michael Caroline, a freshman who was in my ACCESS class, we understand the role confidence plays and the way our capacity in this area grows (as does our commitment) with each subsequent success. While he attributes much of his progress to his improved stamina, the more global gain is in the area of confidence: thanks to his improved speed and stamina, he has more confidence in himself, his ideas, and his abilities.

At the beginning of the year, I never really was into any books and I wasn't really a person who enjoyed reading books. I focused my reading on magazines, comics, newspapers, and easy to read books. I had a hard time choosing the right book for me because it might have been too hard or too boring.

But as it came to mid-December I started to get more into books, such as *Lord of the Flies, The Odyssey,* and *Mice and Men,* which our English class had to read. Also we had to have our own solo book which we had to read and finish in a month and be tested on it, to see if we read it or not. Which also goes for my ACCESS class. As it came to harder books month after month I hated it because they were too long and some of the grammar was a bit difficult. As it came to reading more and more books I started to get into them and started to understand the story.

I learned that reading more books makes your stamina go up, you read more fast and understand the passages more. Reading books made a big improvement in my life and it helped me understand the story more. I became a faster reader, my stamina went up, I started reading more pages as I go on. This book that I was reading at mid April called *Kobe* was a biography of his life and how he got into the NBA at such a young age. This book really changed me as a reader. I understood every single chapter and all the important information which I had never really done before. It was a really big accomplishment for me. As I got tested I did really well and I was really proud of what I did. It was such a great book for me. I did so well on this book because it was a sports biography, which I really get into because I play a lot of sports and I like to know what different skills, and talents these athletes have.

By mid May getting close to the end of my Freshman year, I started to improve on a lot of things such as getting good scores on English assignments, and projects, and speeches. I did well on all these categories. My reading scores went up, my stamina went up a lot. I put more effort on all my assignments and projects. Which all came from my ACCESS class. This really helped me in every subject and on reading books. Though I still struggle on some stuff, I can't be lazy and fool around on any of my subjects, because if I do I will never be successful in life.

Michael reminds us of another critical element of capacity, one that Tom Morris (1994) identifies among his Seven Cs of Success: the capacity for joy.

Michael begins to enjoy his work more and more as his ability to do it improves. As Morris writes, "The only guaranteed way to enjoy success within our lives is to learn to enjoy the process along the way, in its many facets. Dreaming, scheming, striving, wrestling—whatever we are doing at the present moment—can be enjoyed. It need not be just endured as we wait on some future enjoyment that we think some far-off success will bring" (250). This capacity to enjoy is evident among students in my honors English classes; for if they don't love the work, they enjoy the challenge, or find a way to do or think about the work so that they *will* enjoy it. Arthur Eigenbrot, who always came to class early to sneak a few glimpses at the *Guinness Book of World Records*—because he finds information interesting, learning fun—wrote in his letter to incoming freshman, "I think the best way to get the most out of English is to make it fun however you can. Three things that made English fun for me are having reading be something to look forward to, not to groan about; having friends in class to make every day a new adventure; and finally, having an extensive collection of music to listen to while typing essays (this one is crucial if you are to maintain your sanity)."

Another student, Michael Rogers, finds ways to make the assignment his own so he can find it more interesting:

> It's your freshman year; the best advice I can give you is to have fun. In English, you will do nothing but write for the next nine months. Though that might sound dull, it actually provides you with a great opportunity for showing off your character and playing with your literary voice. Don't write those essays just because they are due the next morning; toy around with your writing style. For one essay, play the role of an eloquent scholar describing India's social structure, for the next act like a drunken British intellectual. In these essays, you play the role of the narrator, so the narrator can be anyone you like. To succeed academically, you need to learn how to independently find relationships and connect everything you have learned. Making connections in your studies accounts for a huge amount of time and effort in academia. Have fun with this, too. Don't be afraid to try out some weird connection to see if it works. This is how some of the greatest minds came up with their best ideas!

Another aspect of capacity that merits discussion is tolerance. Some people have more than others; all can improve upon what they have. Two key issues related to tolerance are risk and complexity (or what I might otherwise call the messy simultaneity of school). In his letter, Michael emphasizes the importance of taking intellectual risks, something those with academic confidence can tolerate and for which they are often rewarded. Some risks are social, not intellectual. Priscilla Fernandez, another student in my ACCESS class, wrote, "I took a risk in my history class by asking a question." Such an act represents no danger at all to a student like Michael or Arthur; for Priscilla, however, it shows major academic progress. She says, "In my history class I never asked any questions, but one day I realized that if I asked a question about what I needed to know, it was going to help me in that class. So since then I have been asking questions on what I don't understand. For example on the test reviews, when I ask questions it makes it more easy to study by asking questions."

Priscilla focuses on the tolerance for risk, but freshman Maricela Vega's summary of her day captures the range of demands most students must juggle:

> After class I leave the room and then figure out a way out of school to get to my mother's work. Once I reach her work, I await her signal to tell us where to go. While there I sit and read. After a few hours, we go home and I eat, clean the dishes, everything I have to do before I start my homework. I start with my first class, science, then skip to my third period homework. After I finish these, I continue with my Algebra and English homework. Once finished with all this, I start my daily reading.

Maricela's classmate, Paulina Gavilanez, paints a picture that highlights even more of the demands kids must juggle:

> I wanted to do cross country but it's too late and I don't have any time for it. Maybe, no hopefully, I'll get to do track. I can't really do anything after school because I have to pick up my brother from school and take him to soccer practice. And that ends like at 7:30 then my dad picks us up and then we go home. We get home at 8 or 8:15. Then we eat dinner, we finish at like 9. Go take a 45 minute shower, by that time it's like 9:45. And that's when I start to do my homework. I usually go to bed at 12 or 1 and wake up at 6.
>
> I don't really have time to be with my friends during the weekday or the weekend. And right now I don't even know if I want to have friends. I think I'm fine alone, I'll get things done that way. I don't really want a boyfriend, and in a way I hope I never do. I love my family and I love helping my dad and my mom with my little brother. My parents work a lot, my dad even works on Saturdays, so we are all together on Sunday. I have fun, at home, or during the summer, or when I don't get a lot of homework, then I usually go out with my cousins, or my sort of, might be, not really best friend. But anyway, I'm happy with what I have or the freedom I have.

These two girls, both of whom entered the school through the ACCESS program and went on to college four years later, portray the competing demands in and outside of school. Yet there is an additional level of complexity both teachers and students must have the capacity to manage: the simultaneity within the class itself. Magdalene Lampert (2001) writes:

> One reason teaching [and thus learning] is a complex practice is that many of the problems a teacher must address to get students to learn occur simultaneously, not one after another. . . . When I am teaching fifth-grade mathematics, for example, I teach a mathematical idea or procedure to a student while also teaching that student to be civil to classmates and to me, to complete the tasks assigned, and to think of herself or himself and everyone else in the class as capable of learning, no matter what their gender, race, or parents' income. . . . The study of the practical problems a teacher works on to teach each individual student can not be separate from the study of the practical problems of teaching different kinds of groups or teaching the class as a whole, as all of these elements of the work occur simultaneously in the public space of the classroom. These problems are tackled all at once, by the same person. The work aimed toward accomplishing any single goal of teaching needs to be examined in concert with examining concurrent work, perhaps aimed toward other goals, even toward conflicting goals across the temporal, social, and intellectual problem space in which practice occurs. (3)

It is the inherent and growing complexity of that "problem space" I am talking about as students (and teachers) extend their capacity to do more than one physical and intellectual task at the same time. The swarm of demands, all the more challenging for one with attention difficulties, calls to mind the line, attributed to F. Scott Fitzgerald, about one's intelligence being best measured by a person's ability to think about two mutually exclusive ideas at the same time and still be able to function.

This complexity involves most of the capacities we have discussed. Comparing the complex demands to a tangled ball of yarn we must somehow sort out while doing other things at the same time, we realize that anyone can do it, but some will do it faster than others. Some have the stamina to keep at it longer than others, who may need to work on it for small units of time to maintain their attention. Other capacities are called into action: dexterity, possibly memory (so important to so much of today's academic testing). And joy: some will inevitably find a way to make interesting what is to others a punishing task, showing us all the difference that attitude makes when it comes to work.

I want to end by reiterating the developmental nature of these Four Cs, by emphasizing the idea that the Cs are teachable. Commitment comes through the steady investment in oneself *by* oneself *and* by others. That demonstration of faith in a person's potential, if maintained over time and despite inevitable lapses, creates a context for the content and competence needed to achieve the goals to which one has committed him- or herself. Both content and competence can be developed. While I agree with Yeats that "education is not the filling of a vessel but the lighting of a fire," teachers and students alike must see themselves as vessels capable of holding our culture's most valued knowledge and skills. Then may we light that sacred fire, a fire by which our students can not only warm themselves but guide themselves through the future they must help create while keeping in mind a past they must know, understand, and remember.

I committed myself to lighting this fire not only in my students but in my own three children. Through books, experiences, and mentoring, through my own (and, at home, my wife's) example, and those of others at hand, I share my faith in the future and the role school can play in shaping that future. The teacher I am teaches the students I was, but my son Evan, just now entering middle school, shaped by the culture of a very literate home, is much closer to the student I've become, as his reading autobiography shows:

> Reading is an important part of my family's culture. For as long as I can remember, books have been in every room in our house. My dad is an English teacher and a writer and always has a book in hand. And first thing in the morning I see my mom with the newspaper. So reading became important to me at an early age.
>
> I have been read to most nights of my life. Even though now I read to myself a lot, I still enjoy being read to by my dad. My mom read to me until I was five, then my little brother became old enough to require being read to. My first chapter book was *Charlotte's Web*, then came C. S. Lewis's Narnia books, which my dad read to me. This began the next years of sharing books with my dad. Some of these were Roald Dahl, *The Time Machine, Harry Potter* (all of them!), *A Wrinkle in Time, The Golden Compass*, the *Lord of the Rings* books. My mom enjoys discussing books in her book group and with kids at my brother's school in the Great Books groups. I also like to discuss books.
>
> By being read to I discovered the worlds that books offer. I, like my dad, now almost never go anywhere without a book. And now I am passing down a part of my family culture by sharing books with my younger brother, Whitman.

c c c c

SEVEN

A Practical Postscript
The Four Cs in Action

Of course it's a good idea in practice, Mr. Smith, but will it work in theory?

—punch line to a joke in which a professor spends
the day observing a very successful school program

I once visited a progressive private school whose headmaster described the school's educational philosophy this way: We place our students in the midst of manageable difficulty and then teach them to work their way through it. This is an apt description for the work we do, for its complexity is dynamic, never the same; thus, we face a seemingly endless set of problems we must try to solve. Of these many problems, academic success is a steady customer; the achievement gap seems to be a constant presence, even as we make progress toward closing it. Yet I have outlined in this book some principles that offer useful responses and even solutions to some of these problems if we make intelligent use of the Four Cs to close that gap. Consider this last section a down payment on a larger, more ambitious effort to apply the Four Cs to achieving academic success. In the meantime, here are some ideas administrators and teachers can use to help struggling and successful students alike.

1. Commitment

Administrators show commitment when they effectively address these areas:

• *Professional development:* Invest in quality professional development opportunities throughout the year (including such events as summer institutes to which respected professionals in the field are invited to help motivate and guide teachers). Also, provide scheduled, quality occasions for professional development within departments, between departments, or on subjects of specific interest for school wide groups. Another way you can support (and reward!) your teachers is to send them to professional conventions, especially when they are in your school's region. As part of your commitment to academic success and those kids who have yet to achieve it, always try to send teams of teachers.

- *Strategic planning:* Ask yourself, as part of your planning process for any investment of time, money, or teachers, which of the Four Cs that investment will address. If the investment clearly will make no substantial improvement in any of the Four Cs, either revise the plan so that it does or scrap it and come up with a new plan.

- *Investment:* Assess the levels, types, and sources of commitment in the faculty and build on those people (without burning them out!) and their example to inspire renewed or greater commitment to the school, to teaching, or to students who are not achieving academic success.

- *Culture:* Create and sustain a culture of commitment within the faculty and the school through what you, the faculty, and students do, say, and learn. Challenge, encourage, celebrate, show interest in what teachers and students do.

- *Visitations:* Encourage teachers to tell you when their students are doing work worth coming to watch and celebrate. Go into the classroom to witness the performances, the presentations, the literature circles, the class discussions that give kids (and teachers) a chance to shine.

- *Resources:* Demonstrate your commitment by investing in quality, current materials and resources so students and faculty see that you are committed to ensuring kids get the best education your school can provide. Also, invest in the resources teachers need to do the work you demand; this means not just quality textbooks but up-to-date computers, adequate materials, and universal access to these resources. It also includes students' access to the resources—library, computers, books—they need to succeed; our school, for example, keeps its library open now until 4:30 to ensure all students have access to the Internet, to computers, and to tutors and a space to help them do their work.

- *Reflection:* Read for at least thirty minutes a day in order to maintain and nurture your own commitment to learning and improving. Use these books to nurture your own sense of commitment; read books to help you get and stay committed. A book like *Wall of Fame: One Teacher, One Class, and the Power to Save Schools and Transform Lives* (Freedman 2000) is good medicine; read more practical books like Mike Schmoker's *Results: The Key to Continuous School*

Improvement (1999) to improve your professional knowledge and skills. Discuss what you read with others so that they see that you are committed. For example, reading a book like Donald Phillips' *Lincoln on Leadership* (1993) would expose you to the core principles that made Lincoln such an effective leader in the midst of great and ongoing conflict within and among the people he was elected to lead. Here is the table of contents, which provides useful tips within seconds that can make you more effective in your efforts to help others improve academic success in your school.

PART I: PEOPLE
1. Get Out of the Office and Circulate Among the Troops
2. Build Strong Alliances
3. Persuade Rather Than Coerce

PART II: CHARACTER
4. Honesty and Integrity Are the Best Policies
5. Never Act Out of Vengeance or Spite
6. Have the Courage to Handle Unjust Criticism
7. Be a Master of Paradox

PART III: ENDEAVOR
8. Exercise a Strong Hand—Be Decisive
9. Lead by Being Led
10. Set Goals and Be Results-Oriented
11. Keep Searching Until You Find Your "[Ulysses S.] Grant"
12. Encourage Innovation

PART IV: COMMUNICATION
13. Master the Art of Public Speaking
14. Influence People Through Conversation and Storytelling
15. Preach a Vision and Continually Reaffirm It

• *Programs:* Bring programs to your school that will address the needs of struggling students in proven ways. Programs like AVID, which requires real commitment from everyone at the school, offer guaranteed academic success *for certain students.* Investigate other programs and practices that show potential to meet the needs of other kids. Remember also that it is not enough to bring programs in and assume they will run with the efficiency of self-timed lawn sprinklers; such programs need the right people, ongoing support, and regular professional development (e.g., sending AVID teachers to periodic AVID conferences). Also, it is essential that the people in charge of such programs get the opportunity to explain what the program is and is not, what people should expect and what they should not tolerate. After making such a presentation to the faculty at my school about my own program (ACCESS), my principal wrote the following note, which represents his commitment to the students and the program:

> Jim,
>
> Thank you for the excellent presentation on ACCESS. You covered a lot of ground and gave the staff a clear view of the support ACCESS provides. From the 4 Ps [paper, pencil, photo ID, and planner] to the critical components of academic success, you provided the staff with much "food for thought." I particularly appreciate how you share insight into what allows/supports student success—so important for us all to reflect on that often. Thanks again for your instructional leadership.
>
> —Matt

• *Goals:* Set goals—for yourself, for faculty, for the school, for departments, for students. Then recognize those who reach and surpass those goals.

• *Celebrations:* Celebrate success in any form at any time. My principal started the Rising Star Program, for example, which keeps track of kids' progress from quarter to quarter and gives awards to those students whose overall GPA goes up .5 or more from one progress report to the next (over a six-week period of time).

• *Faith:* Have faith in the course of action you and your faculty choose to follow in order to achieve these academic goals; do not jump from one idea to the next, for such shifting undermines teachers' commitment to your initiatives. Set a goal for the year, one based on evidence and agreed-upon needs; and at year's end, evaluate your progress toward achieving that goal as you revise it for the year ahead. Teachers are much more willing to commit to methods, goals, and programs that will help them solve the problems that prevent them from feeling successful. Our nature is to commit to what will make a difference, which in this case means, whatever will help students succeed in a particular class or school.

• *Feedback:* Provide regular, useful, multiple means of feedback for teachers that they can use to improve instruction and monitor progress. One danger here, though, is spending big money on instruments or programs that teachers do not support and will thus not commit to using in ways that achieve improved academic success.

- *Parents:* Meet with the parents of students at your school who are struggling. My administrators initiated a Latino Parents Group that meets monthly. To this meeting, the administrators invite teachers to explain different aspects of school and how their children can improve. By demonstrating their commitment to their families, their children, and their success, the administrators also show their commitment to the school; at the heart of these meetings, however, is academic success and how students can achieve it.

- *Recognition:* Recognize the efforts, progress, and achievements of individual teachers, students, and departments through personal comments, notes, or announcements. Often the most meaningful recognitions are the private, personal ones. My principal routinely gets out into classrooms and always makes time to write a small note such as the one he wrote after visiting my ACCESS classes one day (see Figure 7.1).

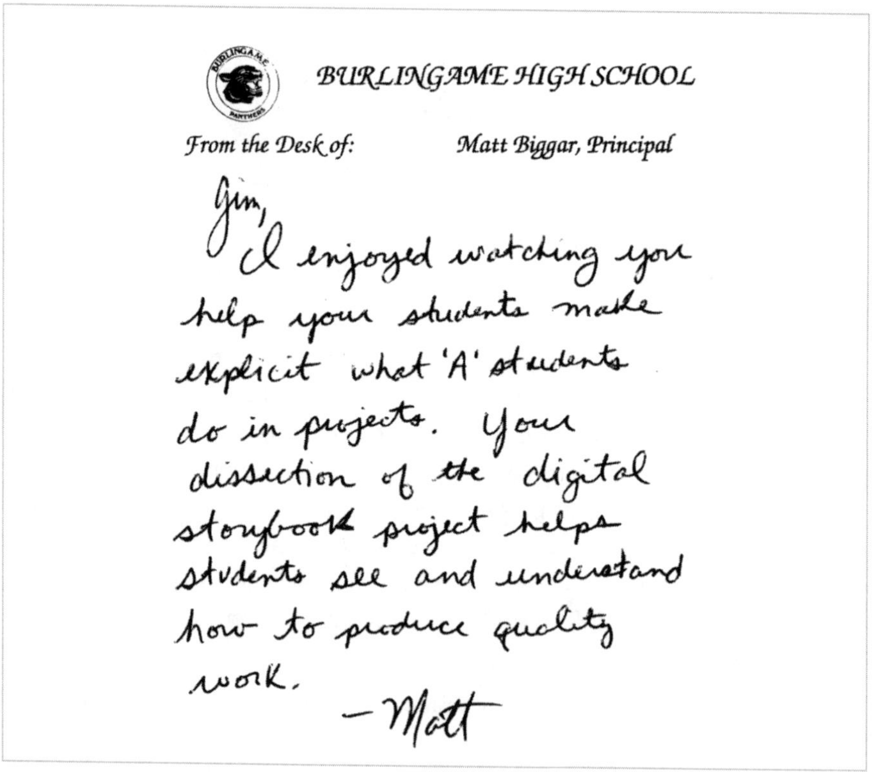

BURLINGAME HIGH SCHOOL

From the Desk of: *Matt Biggar, Principal*

Jim,
I enjoyed watching you help your students make explicit what 'A' students do in projects. Your dissection of the digital storybook project helps students see and understand how to produce quality work.
— Matt

FIGURE 7.1.

Such a note, along with his visit, shows his level of commitment to my work and students' success better than anything else and inspires in me a deeper level of commitment to the school's academic mission.

• *Passion:* Show passion when working on and discussing these issues and ideas. Passion in leaders inspires passion in others; it is infectious. In his book *Leading Minds* (1995), Howard Gardner found that all effective leaders used stories to convey their passion to their constituents in a way that made the constituents want to be a part of that story, to help to make it come true. Administrators who speak from a place of fear—"We have to bring those scores up or they'll close the school!" or "If we don't improve I'll lose my job!"—or obvious personal agenda—"All the other schools in the district improved but us! I can't accept that!"—do not inspire commitment in others. Instead, they inspire resentment and foot-dragging, for the administrator has made it seem like his or her problem and is demanding the teachers solve it. Show passion for kids, for learning, for improving, for teaching, and for teachers. My principal consistently celebrates what we do well and discusses how we do it (which shows he pays attention) even as he encourages us to do better and supports the means we choose to get there. He will, for example, put up on the overhead or publish to the faculty all the positive remarks he heard at Back to School Night; moreover, instead of presenting them as specific to any one teacher, he phrases them in ways that honor the commitment all teachers make to the school and students' success.

• *New Teachers:* Commit to the success of the new teachers. This special plea stems from the crisis in getting and *keeping* qualified, committed new teachers in the profession. When making up a team to go to a convention, be sure to include as many new teachers as possible, in part as a reward and partly as a means of investing in their success.

Teachers show commitment when they concentrate on:

• *Students:* Students want to know that you care about them, that you are invested in their success. Cushman (2003) writes, "Students want teachers to know their strengths and acknowledge their expertise, but they rarely get a chance to make them known" (2). Students are more inclined to be "willing workers" for those teachers who are fair and committed to their success. Caring about them does not mean you need to be their friend; in fact, Cushman found that kids respond more to someone who "knows their stuff" but is approachable. As one kid said, "It's okay if kids hate you at first. If you care about your teaching, we'll get past that" (19). One proviso, however, is that your students must feel (whether it's true or not) that you are committed to them all equally; as soon as they feel that the teacher plays favorites, that teacher's credibility goes out the window. The language teachers use to refer to students figures in prominently; if students feel like they are grouped in the teacher's mind, it undermines their commitment to the teacher and the subject matter, which students feel the teacher has already judged them able or unable to learn.

- *Content:* As the previous entry mentions, kids respond to teachers who know their content, who are committed to the field and subject they are supposed to be able to teach. If teachers don't take the content seriously, why should students? For example, just mentioning books you read outside of school for your own pleasure makes more of an impression than we realize; in *Tuned in and Fired Up,* Sam Intrator (2003) writes, "Mr. Quinn incessantly listened to books on tape and read poetry. He lived with his subject matter in ways that felt authentic to students. As one student said, 'Mr. Quinn loves poetry and writing and it's sort of contagious'" (151).

- *Access:* Everything teachers do must reflect their commitment to helping all students succeed in their class. In *The Competent Classroom* (2001), Zmuda and Tomaino describe a showdown between themselves and their students during which they showed commitment to students' success by asking them what was not working. "A common theme quickly emerged—they were angry with us not because we expected a lot of them, but because they did not understand how to be successful. Frank explained the crux of the matter in his usual blunt fashion: 'Do you really expect us to work hard in here if we know that we are not going to do well?' . . . They did not appreciate or appear to benefit from the drama of training for a goal without knowing what the goal was" (xiv). Commitment to such success means not only being clear about what students must do but providing multiple entry points into or means of completing the assignment that will result in engagement, learning, and further commitment.

- *Culture:* You can taste commitment in the air of some classes. It shows up on the walls, seeps through the words teachers and students use, reveals itself in the way they work. This comes from making room at the table for everyone, creating a culture in which kids' ideas are respected, different perspectives are not just tolerated but welcomed, encouraged. Kids in such a classroom feel safe, alive, like something is going on. Not only does it happen through lively discussions, but it appears on the walls through posted assignments or other visual cues. My classroom, for example, is papered with posters of authors from around the world; kids see that writers and their ideas matter the moment they walk in. They also see photographs of previous students on the walls and immediately sense that the classroom is a community to which they all belong and one to which I am very committed.

- *Consistency:* Everyone can be a heroic teacher for a day or even a week. Commitment demands daily, ongoing, sustained evidence of your devotion to the subject, your goals, and the kids as both people and learners. Inconsistency undermines the teacher's credibility and invites the same level of performance (i.e., "I try only on those things I care about") in students. Consistency refers to quality and effort.

- *Participation:* Teachers show their commitment to the school in many different ways, none of which is more valid than others. Nonetheless, kids do notice and appreciate the efforts teachers make to show their commitment by attending or at least mentioning the student's performance in a recent game or concert or play. Attending events, such as clubs and special weekend events, sends the message to kids, even if the teachers do not attend those events, that they do really care about the school and its students' performance.

- *Reflection:* Success breeds renewed commitment; but one must know they have made progress, that they are doing better than before. Thus effective teachers must create opportunities—after assignments, at week's end, at the end of the grading period or the term—to assess their growth. While such reflection might not improve content knowledge or competence (though if structured right, it can!), it does contribute to the growth of commitment and capacity, especially in the areas of confidence and faith.

2. *Content*

What content looks like for administrators:

- *Professional development:* Teachers need time to learn the latest techniques and information about their profession. Administrators must find ways to provide such professional content knowledge. My first principal, who I should add won the State Principal of the Year Award the year I began teaching, subscribed to some publication called something like *The One-Minute Workshop*. Once a month (or perhaps even more often), every teacher found a small greeting-card-size pamphlet in our mailbox with a specific technique or strategy we could read in the time it took us to walk back to the classroom. Other principals I know buy certain professional books and plant them like seeds, putting them in the hands of teachers they know will read them and who are perhaps doing some work in that area anyway. If money is not available to send teachers to conventions, bring the convention to the school by inviting known speakers to come for the day or hosting a summer institute for which teachers will earn a stipend equivalent to a day's pay. Just as students resent being asked to do assignments without being given good directions or support, teachers resent being asked to do things like improve academic performance for all students without being given the strategies and techniques they need to achieve such ambitious goals. Teachers need teachers, too; even Tiger Woods has a coach, and as someone once told me, "even gold needs to be polished to keep its shine."

- *Conversations:* Called essential conversations, or circles of inquiry, or just plain discussion groups, these groups provide scheduled, structured opportunities for teachers to have the conversations they need about practice. Administrators can contribute to content area knowledge by creating such opportunities (e.g., the third Wednesday of each month instead of a faculty meeting). See the Cycle of Inquiry (Figure 7.2) for examples of what such conversations look like and how they work for both teachers in the classroom and administrators at the schoolwide level.

- *Culture:* Celebrate the importance of what kids study by referring to it, incorporating it into the culture of the school. This culture extends to include the faculty, creating among them a culture of professionalism that honors even as it extends their knowledge of their discipline. Novelist Tobias Wolff's novel *Old School* is set in a school where the "masters" routinely discuss, among themselves and with the students, the importance of ideas, of literature in general and the authors they study in classes. Such a culture within the classrooms and throughout the school charges all that they learn with a sense of importance that makes them want to participate.

What content looks like for teachers:

- *Professional development:* Such professional development might come in the form of attending conferences, but it might just as easily come from reading journals and books, going to museums, attending performances and lectures, or participating in professional discussions with other committed faculty members.

The Classroom Cycle of Inquiry: Planning and Implementing Each Phase

Closing the Achievement Gap in My Classroom

1. Selecting Focal Students' in My Classroom
In my school,
- My school has identified an achievement gap in the academic area of _____. This conclusion is based on data from the following assessments():
- These data reveal an achievement gap of _____ (insert data) between _____ (race/ethnicity) students and _____ (race/ethnicity) students.

My school's target population is therefore _____ (racial or ethnic group).

In my grade level/department...
- Data show that target students at my grade or department level do not meet the following standards in our focus area:

These data come from the following assessments:
- The assessment(s) reveal that target students lack the following skills and subskills necessary to meet our standards:
- If these assessments don't help us identify our target students' skills gaps, we will determine the skills our students lack using the following diagnostic assessments:

In my classroom,
- In my classroom, my focal students, _____ and _____, are members of the target population who need to meet the following standards:
- To do so, they will need to develop the following skills and subskills:

2. Investigating the Effects of My Interaction with Focal Students
- I am challenged when I am interacting with my focal students because...
- I will explore the following resources for ideas about how these challenges might affect my personal interactions with them:
- Aspects of my interaction with them that may be preventing them from acquiring the skills they need are:
- I will examine the following type(s) of interaction with my focal students more fully:
- I will collect data to examine these interactions using the following tools:
- I will meet with my grade/department level colleagues to discuss my findings and get support at the following regular intervals:

3. Identifying Instructional Strategies and Goals
- Right now I use the following instructional strategies to address the above skills with my focal students:
- These practices seem to be helping my students as follows:
- These practices do not seem to be helping my students because:
- My department or grade level has chosen to address my school's achievement gap by focusing on the following instructional strategies:
- Based on research and my teaching experience, I think I will have to adjust these strategies as follows to meet the needs of my focal students:
- My grade level or department will adopt or create the following tool or rubric for the evaluation of these strategies:
- My grade level or department has agreed upon the following picture of effective, high-level implementation of these strategies according to the rubric:
- It is my goal to perform at the following standard on that tool or rubric:

4. Formulating Questions for Inquiry
- My grade level or department needs to determine how effectively our strategies _____ accelerate target student progress and improve their ability to _____
- My grade level/department inquiry question is therefore...
- We will answer this question by comparing our teacher practice data from the tool mentioned above with student achievement data from the following assessments:
- Students will be assessed on the following dates:

5. Setting Measurable Goals for Target Students
- Target students at my grade level/department level will _____
- They will reach this goal by _____ (date).
- My focal students will _____
- They will reach this goal by _____ (date).

6. Examining the Progress of Target Students
- According to the data I am collecting, the strategies I am implementing seem to be working for my focal student(s) _____ because... _____
- They do not seem to be working for my focal student(s) _____ because... _____
- In other classrooms in my department or grade level, focal students are responding to these strategies by...
- We might adjust the strategies by...
- My department or grade level will continue to meet at the following regular intervals to examine target student progress:

7. Examining My Practice and My Interaction with Focal Students
- When I compare the data on my own use of the strategies with my grade level or department's picture of effective implementation, I notice...
- Student achievement and teacher practice data indicate that I might use the strategies more effectively if I...
- My data and my discussions with colleagues suggest that my interactions with focal students...
- I might try altering the nature of my interactions with them to help them learn more by...

8. What We Have Learned: Informing the Whole School Cycle of Inquiry
- Having now carried out both classroom and grade level/department cycles of inquiry, my grade level or department has learned...
- Our findings have the following implications for our whole school cycle of inquiry:
- At classroom, grade level/department or whole school levels, we should now return to step no. _____

' The term "focal students" has been used to refer to those students in a particular teacher's class on whom he or she chooses to conduct inquiry. The term "target students" refers to the racial or ethnic group on which an entire school has chosen to focus its efforts. A teacher's focal students should belong to the target population if possible.

FIGURE 7.2A. The Cycle of Inquiry at the classroom level. Used by permission of the Bay Area School Reform Collaborative.

Cycle of Inquiry

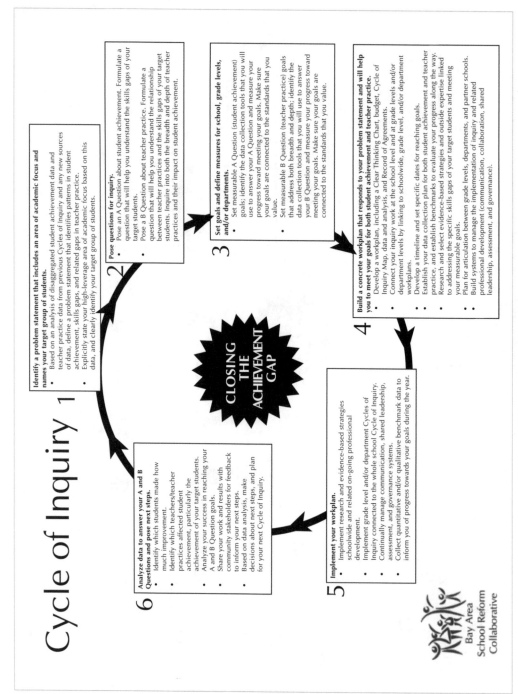

1 Identify a problem statement that includes an area of academic focus and names your target group of students.
- Based on an analysis of disaggregated student achievement data and teacher practice data from previous Cycles of Inquiry and any new sources of data, define a problem statement that identifies patterns in student achievement, skills gaps, and related gaps in teacher practice.
- Explicitly state your high-leverage area of academic focus based on this data, and clearly identify your target group of students.

2 Pose questions for inquiry.
- Pose an A Question about student achievement. Formulate a question that will help you understand the skills gaps of your target students.
- Pose a B Question about teacher practice. Formulate a question that will help you understand the relationship between teacher practices and the skills gaps of your target students. Inquire into both the breadth and depth of teacher practices and their impact on student achievement.

3 Set goals and define measures for school, grade levels, and/or departments.
- Set measurable A Question (student achievement) goals; identify the data collection tools that you will use to answer your A Question and measure your progress toward meeting your goals. Make sure your goals are connected to the standards that you value.
- Set measurable B Question (teacher practice) goals that address both breadth and depth; identify the data collection tools that you will use to answer your B Question and measure your progress toward meeting your goals. Make sure your goals are connected to the standards that you value.

4 Build a concrete workplan that responds to your problem statement and will help you to meet your goals for both student achievement and teacher practice.
- Develop a workplan, including a Clear Thinking Chart, budget, Cycle of Inquiry Map, data and analysis, and Record of Agreements.
- Connect your inquiry work at the school level and at grade levels and/or department levels by linking to schoolwide, grade level, and/or department workplans.
- Develop a timeline and set specific dates for reaching goals.
- Establish your data collection plan for both student achievement and teacher practice, and establish benchmarks to evaluate your progress along the way.
- Research and select evidence-based strategies and outside expertise linked to addressing the specific skills gaps of your target students and meeting your measurable goals.
- Plan for articulation between grade levels, departments, and partner schools.
- Build systems to manage the implementation of inquiry and related professional development (communication, collaboration, shared leadership, assessment, and governance).

5 Implement your workplan.
- Implement research and evidence-based strategies schoolwide and related on-going professional development.
- Implement grade level and/or department Cycles of Inquiry connected to the whole school Cycle of Inquiry. Continually manage communication, shared leadership, assessment, and governance systems.
- Collect quantitative and/or qualitative benchmark data to inform you of progress towards your goals during the year.

6 Analyze data to answer your A and B Questions and pose next steps.
- Identify which students made how much improvement.
- Identify which teachers/teacher practices affected student achievement, particularly the achievement of your target students.
- Analyze your success in reaching your A and B Question goals.
- Share your work and results with community stakeholders for feedback to inform your next steps.
- Based on data analysis, make decisions about next steps, and plan for your next Cycle of Inquiry.

CLOSING THE ACHIEVEMENT GAP

Bay Area School Reform Collaborative

FIGURE 7.2B.   The Cycle of Inquiry at the schoolwide level. Used by permission of the Bay Area School Reform Collaborative.

- *Reading:* Already mentioned, but worth saying more. While I say "reading," I really mean continuing to investigate and generally participate in the ongoing conversation about your particular subject area. Walt Saito, who taught math at Burlingame High School for more than thirty years, traveled to work every day on the train. When asked what he did while on the train (and on weekends, for that matter), Mr. Saito's routine response was "I made up fun new math problems I tried to figure out, of course!" He said it with the same relish a big-game hunter might exude when describing tracking a grizzly bear through the mountains all weekend. If you teach English, it means reading not just professional books but novels, poetry, essays, staying current with new authors, revisiting old authors.

- *Standards:* Simply put, we all need to know the standards for our discipline. They are one means, and an important one, by which we chart the course of our curriculum.

- *Assessment:* Routine assessment before and during a unit ensures that we know what content students know and need to learn and, afterward, how well they learned it and what, if anything, we might need to reteach for better understanding. When it comes to content, we must ask which content they must learn and how best we might teach it; these instructional practices themselves become, inevitably, a part of the content of the course, as do the assessments.

- *Culture:* Included in the culture of the class is the language teachers and students use to discuss what they read, learn, and do. Teachers must teach and consistently use the appropriate academic vocabulary for the content; the vocabulary is part of the content. A crucial part of the culture of any classroom has to do with the issue of engagement and inclusion, by which I mean the extent to which the students connect with the content. Issues of gender, race, ethnicity, ability, and social class are central to this aspect of a class' culture and, to the extent that the teacher makes room for them, form a vital part of the content of the course. In my freshman honors English class, for example, I typically have two-thirds (or more, on occasion) girls. I feel compelled to make sure the subjects we discuss and how we discuss them balance the culture of the class so both sexes feel challenged, included, and respected.

- *Strategic planning:* When you plan your lessons, or a longer unit, begin by asking which of the Four Cs are most lacking or most necessary for success on this assignment. Ask also which of the Four Cs your intended activities, texts, or lessons address; if they do not target any of the Four Cs, ask yourself how you might revise them to include one (or more) of the Cs.

3. Competencies

Given the relationship between content and competency, there is little to list here that does not appear under "Content." There are a few key points to make, however.

What competency looks like for administrators:

- *Professional development:* All such professional development here must relate to improving teachers' skills insofar as they relate to helping students improve theirs. In *The Teaching Gap* (1999), Stigler and Hiebert concentrate on "lesson study," a technique used by Japanese teachers to improve instructional practices as they relate to improving students' academic competence. They meticulously discuss which sequences, which sample problems most effectively teach the skills the students must learn. Thus, administrators should ask themselves if the professional development they are bringing in will, in fact, improve teachers' instructional skills and, more importantly, students' academic skills. While I respect the concept of emotional intelligence, a daylong workshop by an administrator's friend who had begun consulting on EQ offered us nothing we were able to use to improve our teaching in ways that would close the achievement gap or otherwise improve academic performance. This question—which of the Four Cs is this professional development addressing and is it the one we are most concerned about?—is essential to ask when deciding what the faculty needs for professional development. Teachers want to learn, but they want to learn what will help them solve the problems they face each day. Another way to ask this question is, What is the problem for which this professional development activity is the solution?

What competency looks like for teachers:

- *Application:* Students must have the opportunity to apply what they learn if they are to become fluent users of these skills and content. However, real life is much more slippery than most textbooks; thus, kids need to learn how to apply what they learn to a range of increasingly sophisticated problems that ultimately develop their fluency. Again, Stigler and Hiebert (1999) talk about the care with which Japanese teachers select their problems so that that they form a continuum of difficulty; American teachers in most subject areas pose many problems of the same level of difficulty and type, an instructional decision that undermines the development of crucial skills and overall fluency.

- *Reflection:* Another term for this might be *metacognition*, for students (and teachers) must pause to reflect on when, how, and why they use the skills they learned; so, too, must they take time to reflect on how they best learned those skills so they will know how to learn such abilities in the future. For one to become a competent learner, an essential competency in itself, they must routinely consider the process by which they learn. Such a skill is all the more essential in the world students today are preparing to enter tomorrow, for every year brings new tools, new versions of software programs, new procedures by which old tasks are now done.

- *Culture:* The culture of my classroom is built on a foundation of literacy: we read and then use talk and writing to think about what we read, and to communicate with each other, and to develop and convey ideas. Kids know from the first day they come in that these competencies are as essential to their success in the class as is the ability to breathe. Another aspect of this culture is the expectation that they will take their own and others' work seriously; why do work that isn't worth taking seriously? Throughout *An Ethic of Excellence*, Ron Berger (2003) reiterates the importance of culture within a school and a classroom. The word *culture* comes up so constantly in my research and thinking that I consider it the invisible fifth C, for it runs like an underground stream through all the others.

4. Capacity

What capacity looks like for administrators:

- *Materials:* Administrators can ensure that teachers improve students' academic performance by providing materials that will help them do this. A book like *The Reader's Handbook* (Burke 2002), designed to be used in all classes to develop students' reading fluency and comprehension skills, represents such materials. The book develops students' "textual intelligence" (Burke 2001), their capacity to see what a text is made of, to understand how it works, all of which contributes to students' ability to understand what they read. In reading classes, administrators can improve students' speed and stamina by ensuring that appropriately leveled books are available in adequate numbers.

- *Data:* As teachers seek to measure students' improved capacity, they need data provided by a range of effective instruments. This data must also come to teachers in a format that can be quickly digested and put to use. An administrator can provide a binder with one hundred pages of performance data and say they offered to help teachers, but teachers don't have time to digest that and integrate such information into their teaching in a way that makes a difference. Recently my district constructed a common assessment aligned with the state standards to assess students' readiness for the state tests and their overall performance in the areas the test measures. The results were available as a cumulative score, but I could also view an item analysis that showed me which items my students had trouble with; this concise, efficient format allowed me to spend ten minutes reviewing the data and go home with some sense of what I needed to do more work on to improve students' performance. Likewise, content area teachers such as history teachers can review their tests and identify those questions that students commonly missed, then follow up with review not only on the content but the skills needed to succeed on such a test, inviting a discussion about how the students arrived at their answers.

What capacity looks like for teachers:

• *Stamina:* The best example I can offer of what stamina (and speed) look like and how to develop them is the way we handle SSR in my ACCESS class. The kids get a Reading Record sheet (see Figure 6.1) at the beginning of the semester. They read for fifteen minutes four days a week; never fourteen, never sixteen. At the beginning, most of the kids, all of whom are reading several grade levels below ninth grade, can hardly stay focused for three straight minutes. As time goes on, they get up to five, and their speed as measured by the Reading Record shows this progress. Throughout the semester, we use a variety of metacognitive techniques to reflect on why they are reading faster or longer without distraction; this study of their own mind makes them aware of their own processes and helps them to better monitor their own performance. Then we discuss strategies they can use to keep themselves focused when they get frustrated, stuck, bored, or just fatigued. Taking time to examine what happened in kids' minds as they worked through a difficult exam, problem sequence, or equation offers great insight into their minds, insight they can use to improve and become more consistent in their performance as they realize there *are* things they can to do make themselves work and think better.

• *Complexity:* To extend the previous discussion of sustained silent reading, I tell the kids that when they find themselves consistently reading eighteen to twenty pages a day in their SSR book, it is time to reach for a more challenging book. Again, Stigler and Hiebert's (1999) examination of lesson study found that this use of increasingly complex problems was central to students' intellectual growth;

students learned, through the use of these sequentially more complex problems, to be more fluent mathematical thinkers as they tried to use past solutions to solve new and unique problems. The athletic analogy would be weightlifting: one will not get any stronger lifting five-pound weights over and over once they have mastered that amount; to continue to improve, they must move on to seven or ten pounds, pushing the body just past its limits so that it builds capacity. This notion is of vital importance when it comes to the selection of materials and texts to read, for while one might argue merely for engagement, students must also read and work with increasingly difficult texts and tasks if they are to grow intellectually.

• *Feedback:* As we have already discussed, students need feedback on their performance if they are to feel the difference certain techniques make and to see the progress they are making. We do not continue to do what does not appear to work. The feedback must be as immediate as possible and specific to those areas of the performance that the student was learning. Thus, the coach doesn't film the player's whole game, but instead zooms in on the footwork or ball handling the coach is teaching a particular player. The English teacher doesn't (or shouldn't) mark up everything on a paper, but should instead direct his or her attention to the writer's use of adjective clauses or counterarguments or whatever the class was most recently studying.

• *Laughter:* Laughter brings with it energy and a feeling of shared joy. How many classes do students sit in throughout the day and never laugh in? I am not advocating for all of us to become comedians. Indeed, our work is serious, but serious work can still be fun, even funny. Some of the greatest minds, especially among scientists (Einstein and Feynman come to mind), were notorious jokesters. Creative minds need the oxygen that laughter brings.

• *Performances:* Athletes and performers train and rehearse for culminating performances that demand speed, agility, and stamina. Such performances also motivate us to master a song, a script, a move. Students need occasions to which they must rise; such occasions inspire great confidence if the students succeed in doing what they did not think they could do at all. In ACCESS, for example, we work with the Toastmasters International Youth Leadership Program, which requires the kids to give two speeches. They last only two minutes, but they might as well be two hours long as far as the kids are concerned. They lack any faith in their ability to do it; they lack any confidence in themselves as interesting people, often asking why anyone would want to hear what they have to say. And yet when it is over, when they have triumphed, they have a sense of having done something that gives them the confidence they need to do other things.

- *Speed:* In this era of high-stakes testing, speed unfortunately matters. One thing I do as we get closer to testing season is practice quick starts and discuss how to prioritize time when taking the test. It is a bit like the scene in *Seabiscuit* when they gather on the racetrack late at night and train the horse to start fast at the sound of the bell. Of course I don't like comparing my students to horses, but this is Seabiscuit we are talking about, a true winner, an elite athlete who spent most of his life only five miles from where I teach. As time allows, we will try to debrief after they finish with the quick start on the essay, asking what techniques they used, which questions they asked to help them get started, or why they had so much difficulty getting started. Such discussions are important, for they yield revealing comments such as one from a girl who wrote that she had not put anything down after ten minutes because everything she had to say was stupid, that all she could hear was her mother telling her how dumb she was; with this out in the open, I could tell her to try it again, and this time around she launched into her paper with ease, guided by my words about her intelligence instead of her mother's insults.

All of these suggestions are guided by the desire to help students learn to live and thrive in the schoolhouse. As Keith Devlin (2000) says of learning mathematics:

> When we enter a house for the first time, we of course find it unfamiliar. By walking around for a while, however, looking into various rooms and peering into cupboards, we quickly get to know it. But what if we cannot enter the house, and our only knowledge of it comes from the instructions and plans that were used to build it? Moreover, what if those instructions and plans are written in a highly technical language that we find intimidating and incomprehensible? What if, try as we may, we cannot form any mental picture of the house? Then we are not going to get much of a sense of what it is like to live there. We are not going to be able to enter the house even in our imagination. (128)

School, ideas, texts, micro- and macroscopic worlds, the present and past, as well as the future—these are just some of the many different houses that we are trying to help our students live in, to move around in with ease so that they might feel at home in the world that we hope they will be able to help govern, protect, and ultimately, create.

APPENDIX A
Works Cited

Adler, Mortimer. 1982. *The Paideia Proposal: An Educational Manifesto*. New York: Collier.

American Federation of Teachers. 1999. "Lessons from the World: What TIMSS Tells Us About Mathematics Achievement, Curriculum, and Instruction." *Educational Policy Issues Policy Brief* 10.

Applebee, Arthur. 1996. *Curriculum as Conversation: Transforming Traditions of Teaching and Learning*. Chicago: University of Chicago Press.

Bennett, William, ed. 1996. *The Book of Virtues: A Treasury of Great Moral Stories*. New York: Touchstone.

Berger, Ron. 2003. *An Ethic of Excellence: Building a Culture of Craftsmanship with Students*. Portsmouth, NH: Heinemann.

Black, Laurel Johnson. 1995. "This Fine Place So Far from Home: Voices of Academics from the Working Class." In *This Fine Place So Far from Home: Voices of Academics from the Working Class*, ed. C. L. Barney, Law Dews, and Carolyn Leste. Philadelphia: Temple University Press.

Bloom, Benjamin. 1956. *Taxonomy of Educational Objectives: The Classification of Educational Goals: Handbook I, Cognitive Domain*. New York; Toronto: Longmans; Green.

Boiarsky, Carolyn. 2003. *Academic Literacy in the English Class*. Portsmouth, NH: Heinemann.

Bradley, Bill. 1998. *Values of the Game*. New York: Broadway.

Brandt, Deborah. 2001. *Literacy in American Lives*. Cambridge: Cambridge University Press.

Breuggemann, Walter. 1995. *Praying the Psalms*. Winona, MN: St. Mary's.

Brown, Rexford. 1993. *Schools of Thought: How the Politics of Literacy Shape Thinking in the Classroom*. San Francisco: Jossey-Bass.

Burke, Jim. 2001. *Illuminating Texts.* Portsmouth: Heinemann.

———. 2002. *The Reader's Handbook: A Student Guide for Reading and Learning.* Wilmington, MA: Great Source.

———. 2003. *The English Teacher's Companion: A Complete Guide to Classroom, Curriculum, and the Profession,* Second Edition. Portsmouth, NH: Heinemann.

———. 2004. *The Teacher's Daybook 2004–2005: Time to Teach • Time to Learn • Time to Live.* Portsmouth, NH: Heinemann.

Caine, Renate Nummela, and Geoffrey Caine. 1994. *Making Connections: Teaching and the Human Brain.* Menlo Park, CA: Addison-Wesley.

Center on English Learning and Achievement. 2003. "Tracking and the Literacy Gap." *English Update: A Newsletter from the Center on English Learning and Achievement* spring: 8.

Clark, Ron. 2003. *The Essential 55: An Award-Winning Educator's Rules for Discovering the Successful Student in Every Child.* New York: Hyperion.

Conley, David T. 2003. *Understanding University Success: A Report for Success.* Eugene, OR: Center for Educational Policy Research (www.s4s.org).

Costa, Arthur, and Bena Ballick. 2000. *Habits of Mind,* ed. Arthur Costa and Bena Ballick. Alexandria, VA: Association for Supervision and Curriculum Development.

Costa, Arthur, and Robert Garmston. 2001. "Five Human Passions: The Origins of Effective Thinking." In *Developing Minds: A Resource Book for Teaching Thinking,* ed. Arthur Costa. Alexandria, VA: Association for Supervision and Curriculum Development.

Csikszentmihalyi, Mihaly. 1991. *Flow: The Psychology of Optimal Experience.* New York: HarperPerennial.

———. 1996. *Creativity: Flow and the Psychology of Discovery and Invention.* New York: HarperPerennial.

Csikszentmihalyi, Mihalyi, and Barbara Schneider. 2000. *Becoming Adult: How Teenagers Prepare for the World of Work.* New York: Basic.

Cushman, Kathleen. 2003. *Fires in the Bathroom: Adivce for Teachers from High School Students.* New York: New.

Delpit, Lisa. 1995. *Other People's Children: Cultural Conflict in the Classroom.* New York: New.

DeStigter, Todd. 2001. *Reflections of a Citizen Teacher: Literacy, Democracy, and the Forgotten Students of Addison High.* Urbana, IL: National Council of Teachers of English.

Devlin, Keith. 2000. *The Math Gene: How Mathematical Thinking Evolved and Why Numbers Are Like Gossip.* New York: Basic.

Doyle, Denis. 2003. "Letter from Washington." *Educational Leadership* January: 96.

Fielding, Audrey, Ruth Schoenbach, and Marean Jordan. 2003. *Building Academic Literacy: Lessons from Reading Apprenticeship Classrooms, 6–12.* San Francisco: Jossey-Bass.

Freedman, Jonathan. 2000. *Wall of Fame: One Teacher, One Class, and the Power to Save Schools and Transform Lives.* San Diego: Avid Academic and San Diego State University Press.

Friedman, Thomas L. 1992. *The Lexus and the Olive Tree: Understanding Globalization.* New York: Anchor.

Friere, Paolo. 1993. *Pedagogy of the Oppressed.* New York: Continuum.

Gardner, Howard. 1991. *The Unschooled Mind: How Children Think and How Schools Should Teach.* New York: Basic Books.

———. 1992. *Frames of Mind: The Theory of Multiple Intelligences.* New York: Basic.

———. 1993. *Multiple Intelligences: The Theory in Practice: A Reader.* New York: Basic.

———. 1995. *Leading Minds: An Anatomy of Leadership.* New York: Basic.

———. 1999. *The Disciplined Mind: Beyond Facts and Standardized Tests, the K–12 Education That Every Child Deserves.* New York: Simon and Schuster.

Geertz, Clifford. 1973. *The Interpretation of Cultures.* New York: Basic.

Gilster, Paul. 1997. *Digital Literacy.* New York: Wiley Computer.

Goslin, David. 2003. "Student Engagement." *Education Week* 23 (8): 32, 34.

Graff, Gerald. 2003. *Clueless in Academe: How Schooling Obscures the Life of the Mind.* New Haven: Yale University Press.

Greer, Colin, and Herbert Kohl. 1995. *A Call to Character: A Family Treasury.* New York: Harper Collins.

Hirsch, E. D. 1988. *Cultural Literacy: What Every American Needs to Know.* New York: Houghton Mifflin.

Hrabowski, Freeman A., Kenneth I. Maton, and Geoffrey L. Greif. 1998. *Beating the Odds: Raising Academically Successful African American Males.* New York: Oxford University Press.

Intersegmental Committee of Academic Senates (ICAS). 2002. *Academic Literacy: A Statement of Competencies Expected of Students Entering California's Public Colleges and Universities.* Sacramento: ICAS.

Intrator, Sam. 2003. *Tuned in and Fired Up: How Teaching Can Inspire Real Learning in the Classroom.* New Haven: Yale University Press.

Intrator, Sam, and Megan Scribner. 2003. *Teaching with Fire: Poetry That Sustains the Courage to Teach.* San Francisco: Jossey-Bass.

Jago, Carol. 2001. "Something There Is That Does't Love a List." *American Educator.*

Kiyosaki, Robert T. 1997. *Rich Dad, Poor Dad: What the Rich Teach Their Kids About Money—That the Poor and Middle Class Do Not!* New York: Warner.

Klemp, Ron. 2003. "Academic Literacy: Making Students Content Area Learners." Wilmington, MA: Great Source.

Kozol, Jonathan. 1992. *Savage Inequalities: Children in America's Schools.* New York: Perennial.

Lampert, Magdalene. 2001. *Teaching Problems and the Problems of Teaching.* New Haven: Yale University Press.

Langer, Judith. 1991. "Literacy and Schooling: A Sociocognitive Perspective." In *Literacy for a Diverse Society: Perspectives, Practices, and Policies*, ed. Elfrieda H. Heibert, 316. New York: Teachers College Press.

———. 1995. *Envisioning Literature: Literary Understanding and Literature Instruction.* New York: Teachers College Press/International Reading Association..

———. 2002. *Effective Literacy Instruction: Building Successful Reading and Writing Programs.* Urbana, IL: National Council of Teachers of English.

———. 2003. "The Literate Mind." *English Update* spring: 4–7.

LePell, Clare. 2003. Personal letter, 20 December.

Levine, Mel. 1994. *Educational Care: A System for Understanding and Helping Children with Learning Problems at Home and in School.* Cambridge: Educators Publishing Service, Inc.

———. 2002. *A Mind at a Time: America's Top Learning Expert Shows How Every Child Can Succeed.* New York: Simon and Schuster.

———. 2003. *The Myth of Laziness: America's Top Learning Expert Shows How Kids—and Parents—Can Become More Productive.* New York: Simon and Schuster.

Light, Richard J. 2001. *Making the Most of College: Students Speak Their Minds.* Cambridge: Harvard University Press.

Loehr, Jim, and Tony Schwartz. 2003. *The Power of Full Engagement: Managing Energy, Not Time, Is the Key to High Performance and Personal Renewal.* New York: Free Press.

Marzano, Robert J. 1991. *Cultivating Thinking in English and the Language Arts.* Urbana, IL: National Council of Teachers of English, 1991.

———. 2001. *Designing a New Taxonomy of Educational Objectives*, ed. Thomas R. Guskey and Robert J. Marzano. Thousand Oaks, CA: Corwin.

Marzano, Robert J., Debra J. Pickering, and Jane E. Pollack. 2001. *Classroom Instruction That Works: Research-Based Strategies for Increasing Student Achievement.* Alexandria, VA: Association for Supervision and Curriculum Development.

Mathews, Jay. 1988. *Escalante: The Best Teacher in America*. New York: Henry Holt.

Meier, Deborah. 2001. *In Schools We Trust: Creating Communities of Learning in an Era of Testing and Standardization*. Boston: Beacon.

Millard, Elaine. 1997. *Differently Literate: Boys, Girls, and the Schooling of Literacy*. London: Falmer.

Mooney, Jonathan, and David Cole. 2000. *Learning Outside the Lines: Two Ivy League Students with Learning Disabilities and ADHD Give You the Tools for Academic Success and Educational Revolution*. New York: Fireside.

Morris, Tom. 1994. *True Success: A New Philosophy of Excellence*. New York: Berkley.

Moses, Robert, and Charles E. Cobb. 2001. *Math Literacy and Civil Rights*. Boston: Beacon.

Murnane, Richard J., and Frank Levy. 1996. *Teaching the New Basic Skills: Principles for Educating Children to Thrive in a Changing Economy*. New York: Free.

Myers, Miles. 1996. *Changing Our Minds: Negotiating English and Literacy*. Urbana, IL: National Council of Teachers of English.

National Board for Professional Teaching Standards (NBPTS). 2003. *Adolescence and Young Adulthood/English Language Arts Standards*. Arlington: NBPTS.

Newkirk, Tom. 1997. *The Performance of Self in Student Writing*. Portsmouth, NH: Heinemann.

———. 2003. "Quiet Crisis in Boys' Literacy." *Education Week* 23 (2): 34.

Noguera, Pedro A. 2003. "Joaquim's Dilemma: Understanding the Link Between Racial Identity and School-Related Behaviors." In *Adolescents at School: Perspectives on Youth, Identity, and Education,* ed. Michael Sadowski. Cambridge: Harvard Education Press.

Olson, Carol Booth. 2002. *The Reading/Writing Connection: Strategies for Teaching and Learning in the Secondary Classroom*. Boston: Allyn and Bacon.

Osborn, Michael, and Suzanne Osborn. 1997. *Public Speaking*. 3rd ed. Boston: Houghton Mifflin Co.

Perry, Theresa, Claude Steele, and Asa Hilliard III. 2003. *Young, Gifted, and Black: Promoting High Achievement Among African-American Students*. Boston: Beacon.

Phillips, Donald. 1993. *Lincoln on Leadership: Executive Strategies for Tough Times*. New York: Warner.

Pope, Denise Clark. 2001. *"Doing School": How We Are Creating a Generation of Stressed Out, Materialistic, and Miseducated Students*. New Haven: Yale University Press.

Public Agenda. 1999. "Employer and Professor Evaluation of Students' Skills."

Ravitch, Diane. 2003. *The Language Police: How Pressure Groups Restrict What Students Learn*. New York: Alfred A. Knopf.

Reich, Robert. 1992. *The Work of Nations: Preparing Ourselves for the Twenty-First Century.* New York: Vintage.

Resnick, Lauren. 1999. "Making America Smarter." *Education Week* 18 (40): 38–40.

Rich, Dorothy. 1997. *Megaskills: Building Children's Achievement for the Information Age.* Boston: Houghton Mifflin.

Ritchhart, Ron. 2002. *Intellectual Character: What It Is, Why It Matters, and How to Get It.* San Francisco: Jossey-Bass.

Rose, Mike. 1989. *Lives on the Boundary: A Moving Account of the Struggles and Achievements of America's Educational Underclass.* New York: Penguin.

Schmoker, Mike. 1999. *Results: The Key to Continuous School Improvement.* Alexandria, VA: Association of Supervision and Curriculum Development.

Schoenbach, Ruth, Cynthia Greenleaf, Christine Cziko, and Lori Hurwitz. 1999. *Reading for Understanding: A Guide to Improving Reading in Middle and High School Classrooms.* San Francisco: Jossey-Bass.

Simon, Katherine G. 2001. *Moral Questions in the Classroom: How to Get Kids to Think Deeply About Real Life and Their Schoolwork.* New Haven: Yale University Press.

Sizer, Ted, and Nancy Faust Sizer. 1999. *The Students Are Watching: Schools and the Moral Contract.* Boston: Beacon.

Smith, Frank. 1988. *Joining the Literacy Club: Further Essays into Education.* Portsmouth, NH: Heinemann.

Smith, Michael, and Jeff Wilhelm. 2002. *Reading Don't Fix No Chevys: Literacy in the Lives of Young Men.* Portsmouth, NH: Heinemann.

Springer, G. T. 2003. Personal correspondence. 20 November.

Stevenson, Harold W., and James W. Stigler. 1992. *The Learning Gap: Why Our Schools Are Failing and What We Can Learn from Japanese and Chinese Education.* New York: Touchstone.

Stigler, James W., and James Hiebert. 1999. *The Teaching Gap: Best Ideas from the World's Teachers for Improving Education in the Classroom.* New York: Free Press.

Stotsky, Sandra. 1999. *Losing Our Language: How Multicultural Classroom Instruction Is Undermining Our Children's Ability to Read, Write, and Reason.* New York: Free Press.

Suarez-Orozco, Marcelo, and Howard Gardner. 2003. "Educating Billy Wong for the World of Tomorrow." *Education Week* 23 (8): 42, 44.

Suskind, Ron. 1998. *A Hope in the Unseen: An American Odyssey from the Inner City to the Ivy League.* New York: Broadway.

Sykes, Charles J. 1995. *Dumbing Down Our Kids: Why American Children Feel Good About Themselves But Can't Read, Write, or Add.* New York: St. Martin's Griffin.

Tomlinson, Carol Ann. 1999. *The Differentiated Classroom: Responding to the Needs of All Learners.* Alexandria, VA: Association of Supervision and Curriculum Development.

Tucker, Marc S., and Judy B. Codding. 1998. *Standards for Our Schools: How to Set Them, Measure Them, and Reach Them.* San Francisco: Jossey-Bass.

U.S. Department of Labor. 1991. *Secretary's Commission on Achieving Necessary Skills (SCANS) Report: What Work Requires of Schools.* Washington, DC: U.S. Department of Labor.

Viadero, Debra. 2003. "Self-Defeating Behaviors." *Education Week* 22 (28): 8.

Wilhelm, Jeff. 2003. Reports from Cyberspace. Paper presented at the National Council of Teachers of English, San Francisco, 9 November.

Wisconsin Center for Education Research. 2002. "Measuring the Content of Instruction." *Wisconsin Center for Education Research Highlights* 14 (4): 1.

Wolff, Tobias. 2003. *Old School.* New York: Alfred A. Knopf.

Wong, William. 2001. "Taking the Measure of Our Children." *San Francisco Chronicle* 19 March, A21.

Wooden, John. 1988. *They Call Me Coach.* Chicago: Contemporary.

Zmuda, Allison, and Mary Tomaino. 2001. *The Competent Classroom: Aligning High School Curriculum, Standards, and Assessment—A Creative Teaching Guide.* New York: Teachers College Press/National Education Association.

Zuboff, Shoshanna. 1989. *In the Age of Smart Machines: The Future of Work and Power.* Boston: Basic Books.

APPENDIX B
Executive Summary

This document reports what faculty from all three segments of California's system of higher education think about their students' ability to read, write, and think critically. It echoes the lucid arguments made for literacy in the *Statement of Competencies in English Expected of Freshmen*, which appeared in 1982, but it necessarily revises and updates that earlier document. In the past two decades, California's educational landscape has been swept by substantial changes in pedagogy, advances in technology, and new emphases on critical reading, writing, and thinking across the curriculum. These changes have transformed the field, and they have shaped this report in ways that could not have been foreseen twenty years ago.

Like the earlier report, this document was produced by a faculty task force appointed by the Intersegmental Committee of Academic Senates (ICAS), which is comprised of the Academic Senates of the University of California, the California State University, and the California Community Colleges. Unlike that earlier document, this report is based upon the responses of faculty from many disciplines requiring students to read, write, and think critically. The task force invited faculty who regularly teach introductory or first-year courses to participate in a Web-based interview study that asked the following questions. (A transcription of that survey appears in the appendices.)

- What do they expect of their students' reading, writing, and critical thinking?
- How well are their students prepared for those expectations, and why or why not?
- How do they expect their students to acquire these skills, experiences, or competencies that they are missing at matriculation?

We also asked those faculty to identify other factors that contributed to their students' academic success:

- What attitudes or predispositions—"habits of mind"—facilitate student learning?
- What kinds of technology do faculty use or intend soon to use with their own classes?

This report summarizes responses to these questions and describes patterns that emerged in the answers. It then combines our colleagues' views with research and our collective professional experience to produce specific recommendations that will improve the level of literacy among first-year students in all segments of higher education in our state.

Contents of This Report

The statement is divided into three parts, followed by appendices:

- Part I. Academic Literacy: Reading, Writing, and Thinking Critically: discusses expectations and perceived student preparation and provides a rationale for these competencies understood as larger, more holistic "abilities" rather than a list of discrete "skills."

- Part II. Competencies: charts the competencies of Part I and juxtaposes them with comparable competencies noted in the California Language Arts Content Standards and in the California Education Roundtable Content Standards.

- Part III. Strategies for Implementation: offers suggestions for "teaching the processes of learning."

A Selection of Significant Findings and Recommendations Contained Within This Statement

ACADEMIC LITERACY ACROSS THE CONTENT AREAS

- We affirm the role of California schools in enhancing democracy, and we believe that literacy skills serve as the foundation for greater equity.

- All the elements of academic literacy—reading, writing, listening, speaking, critical thinking, use of technology, and habits of mind that foster academic success—are expected of entering freshmen across all college disciplines. These competencies should be learned in the content areas in high school. It is, therefore, an institutional obligation to teach them.

• In order to be prepared for college and university courses, students need greater exposure to and instruction in academic literacy than they receive in English classes alone. This need calls for greater coordination of literacy education among subject matter areas within high schools.

• The inseparable skills of critical reading, writing, listening, and thinking depend upon students' ability to postpone judgment and tolerate ambiguity as they honor the dance between passionate assertion and patient inquiry.

• We applaud recent efforts towards collaboration and articulation between high schools and colleges and urge that these efforts be continued and expanded.

• We recommend imaginative and practical professional development as a central component of improving literacy education.

HABITS OF MIND AND CRITICAL THINKING

• The habits of mind expected of students—their curiosity, their daring, their participation in intellectual discussions—are predicated upon their ability to convey their ideas clearly and to listen and respond to divergent views respectfully.

• Faculty expect students to have an appetite to experiment with new ideas, challenge their own beliefs, seek out other points of view, and contribute to intellectual discussions.

• Analytical thinking must be taught, and students must be encouraged to apply those analytical abilities to their own endeavors as well as to the work of others.

• Students should generate critical responses to what they read, see, and hear, and develop a healthy skepticism toward their world.

• Students must assume a measure of responsibility for their own learning, must discern crucial values of the academic community, must seek assistance when they need it, and must advocate for their own learning in diverse situations.

• Self-advocacy is a valuable practice that emerges from the recognition that education is a partnership.

READING AND WRITING CONNECTION

• College faculty report that student reading and writing are behaviors and that, as such, they are interpreted as evidence of attitudes regarding learning.

The Executive Summary of Academic Literacy: A Statement of Competencies Expected of Students Entering California's Public Colleges and Universities. © 2000 by Intersegmental Committee of the Academic Senates (ICAS); Sacramento, CA; www.academicsenate.cc.ca.us. Reprinted with permission.

- Successful students understand that reading and writing are the lifeblood of educated people.

- Students, like the writers whose works they read, should articulate a clear thesis and should identify, evaluate, and use evidence to support or challenge that thesis while being attentive to diction, syntax, and organization.

- Students who need help overcoming their lack of preparation will generally need to engage in practices of self-advocacy, including finding campus instructional resources on their own.

READING

- 83% of faculty say that the lack of analytical reading skills contributes to students' lack of success in a course.

- Faculty respondents concur with the California Education Round Table (CERT) standards which, unlike the California Language Arts Standards, call for students' comprehension of "academic and workplace texts."

- Reading is generally not formally taught after a certain point in students' K–12 education.

- Teachers in all disciplines must help students develop effective critical reading strategies.

- We must teach our students to be active makers of meaning and teach them the strategies all good readers employ: to think critically, to argue, to compare, to own an idea, and to remember. Reading is a process that requires time and reflection, and that stimulates imagination, analysis, and inquiry.

WRITING

- Only $\frac{1}{3}$ of entering college students are sufficiently prepared for the two most frequently assigned writing tasks: analyzing information or arguments and synthesizing information from several sources, according to faculty respondents.

- More than 50% of their students fail to produce papers relatively free of language errors, according to our faculty respondents.

- Faculty judge students' ability to express their thinking clearly, accurately, and compellingly through their writing. College faculty look for evidence in papers that students are stretching their minds, representing others' ideas responsibly, and exploring ideas.

The Executive Summary of Academic Literacy: A Statement of Competencies Expected of Students Entering California's Public Colleges and Universities. © 2000 *by Intersegmental Committee of the Academic Senates (ICAS); Sacramento, CA; www.academicsenate.cc.ca.us. Reprinted with permission.*

- In college, students may well be asked to complete complex writing tasks across the disciplines with little instruction provided.

- Faculty expect students to reexamine their thesis, to consider and reconsider additional points or arguments, to reshape and reconstruct as they compose, and to submit carefully revised and edited work.

- College faculty assign writing to get to know how students think, to help students engage critically and thoughtfully with course readings, to demonstrate what students understand from lectures, to structure and guide their inquiry, to encourage independent thinking, and to invite them into the on-going intellectual dialogue that characterizes higher education. Writing in college is designed to deepen and extend discourse in the pursuit of knowledge.

- In the last two years of high school, students need to be given instruction in writing in *every* course and to be assigned writing tasks that

   - demand analysis, synthesis, and research;

   - require them to generate ideas for writing by using texts in addition to past experience or observations; and

   - require students to revise to improve focus, support, and organization, and to edit or proofread to eliminate errors in grammar, mechanics, and spelling.

- Implementation of strong writing-across-the-curriculum programs in high schools statewide can help prepare high school students for their writing requirements in college.

LISTENING AND SPEAKING

- Students are expected to speak with a command of English language conventions.

- All students who enter college without having developed essential critical listening skills or who have not had ample practice speaking in large and small groups will find themselves disadvantaged.

- The California English Language Arts Content Standards [on listening and speaking], if regularly addressed and evaluated in the years before high school graduation, would equip entering college students to perform requisite listening and speaking tasks.

The Executive Summary of Academic Literacy: A Statement of Competencies Expected of Students Entering California's Public Colleges and Universities. © *2000 by Intersegmental Committee of the Academic Senates (ICAS); Sacramento, CA; www.academicsenate.cc.ca.us. Reprinted with permission.*

- College-level work requires students to be active, discerning listeners in lecture and discussion classes and to make critical distinctions between key points and illustrative examples, just as they must do when they read and write.

ENGLISH LANGUAGE LEARNERS (L2 LEARNERS)

- Language minority students comprise nearly 40% of all K–12 students in California.

- The dominant perception among faculty respondents is that many L2 students are not prepared to meet college-level academic demands.

- Academic English involves dispositions and skills beyond those of conversational fluency. Classification of L2 students as FEP (fluent English proficient) is best determined by assessment of the multiple abilities necessary in academic situations: reading, writing, listening, and speaking.

- "ESL" is faculty short hand for many types of students, regardless of their varying language problems and backgrounds. Yet all second language learners are expected to control the same set of competencies for success as other students upon entering postsecondary institutions.

- To provide appropriate instruction for each individual L2 learner, we must recognize the different subgroups of second language learners, distinguished primarily by such differences as

  - length of residence in the U.S.,
  - years of U.S. schooling, and
  - English language proficiency, both oral and written.

- L2 students who have received most, if not all, of their education in California schools may continue to have special *academic* literacy needs. Thus, specialized college or university instruction in academic English is both desirable and necessary, and additional time may be required to complete requirements essential for success at the baccalaureate level.

- L2 learners, their peers, parents, teachers, and administrators should come to understand that special language instruction is not remedial. Given this awareness, L2 students will be more likely to further develop academic English through ESL work at the college level.

TECHNOLOGY

- Students' success in college has as much to do with their ability to find information as to recall it.

- While many entering students are familiar with some technological elements (notably e-mail and Web browsing), few demonstrate the crucial ability to evaluate online resources critically.

- Students need to form questioning habits when they read, especially material found on the Internet where students must evaluate materials for clarity, accuracy, precision, relevance, depth, breadth, logic, significance, and fairness.

- Technological skills and students' critical appraisal of them should also be taught across the curriculum.

- Students should enter with basic technological skills that include word processing, e-mail use, and the fundamentals of Web-based research. All students, therefore, should have regular access to computers.

The Executive Summary of Academic Literacy: A Statement of Competencies Expected of Students Entering California's Public Colleges and Universities.© *2000 by Intersegmental Committee of the Academic Senates (ICAS); Sacramento, CA; www.academicsenate.cc.ca.us. Reprinted with permission.*

Index